IT'S ONLY MONEY

CW00551835

IT'S ONLY MONEY

Peter Pugh

ICON BOOKS

Published in the UK in 2006 by
Icon Books Ltd, The Old Dairy,
Brook Road, Thriplow,
Cambridge SG8 7RG
email: info@iconbooks.co.uk
www.iconbooks.co.uk

Sold in the UK, Europe, South Africa and Asia
by Faber & Faber Ltd, 3 Queen Square,
London WC1N 3AU
or their agents

Distributed in the UK, Europe, South Africa and Asia
by TBS Ltd, TBS Distribution Centre, Colchester Road
Frating Green, Colchester CO7 7DW

Published in Australia in 2006
by Allen & Unwin Pty Ltd,
PO Box 8500, 83 Alexander Street,
Crows Nest, NSW 2065

Distributed in Canada by
Penguin Books Canada,
90 Eglinton Avenue East, Suite 700,
Toronto, Ontario M4P 2YE

ISBN-10: 1-84046-738-X
ISBN-13: 978-1840467-38-3

Typesetting by Hands Fotoset

Printed and bound in the UK by
Bookmarque Ltd

Contents

About the author

Peter Pugh is the author of over 40 books on business, including the first book about the Guinness scandal of the 1980s and an official three-volume history of Rolls-Royce. He has also written titles for Icon's *Introducing* series on John Maynard Keynes and Margaret Thatcher, and a biography of the legendary Barnes Wallis.

Model Linda Evangelista famously said: 'I don't get out of bed for less than $10,000.'

How much do you get out of bed for?

If you're on the minimum wage and an eight-hour day, it's £40.40.

If you're in the City and earn £200,000 a year with a Christmas bonus of £1 million, it's £4,615.

If you're Rio Ferdinand it's £22,000.

If you're a reasonably well-paid teacher on £30,000 a year it's £115.

If you're Philip Green and pay yourself £1.2 billion a year, it's £4,615,384.

If you're the Governor of the Bank of England it's £1,031 and 30 pence, to be precise.

If you're the boss of Goldman Sachs, the American investment bank, it's £80,769.

This book is about money. We all, or nearly all of us, have to think about money almost all of the time. Perhaps the only people who don't think about money are not the very rich, most of whom seem obsessed with the worry of losing it, but the very, very poor in remote parts of the world where there is no money.

However, most of us find money and talk of it either boring or somehow intimidating. Most people feel that they aren't paid as much as they should be, or that they don't accumulate as much as they should. They don't care that they are very rich compared with the millions in Africa who subsist on less than $1 a day. They can't relate to that. What they can relate to is those around them, most of whom seem to earn more for doing less.

In the UK, people with salaries of £30–35,000 think of themselves as 'middle income' without realising that 90 per cent of taxpayers earn less. Envy is rife and is constantly exploited by politicians. There are very few main board directors of the top 100 companies, but they do earn £10,000 more than a waitress – and that's not per year, that's £10,000 more per *week*!

Although this is a book about money, you will not find it threatening nor, I hope, boring. Many of the anecdotes will surprise you and some will amuse you. A number of them do relate to the change in what a £ or $ will buy, and we therefore need some measure of inflation.

There are a number of formulas used to calculate inflation, such as the Retail Price Index, but I think we should use the following, which is based on the average working wage.

There was little inflation in the UK until the 20th century. Therefore, anything up to 1900 and the early 20th century – multiply by 110 to equate with today's prices;
1918–45 – multiply by 55 to equate to today's prices;
1945–50 – multiply by 30 to equate to today's prices;
1950–60 – multiply by 25 to equate to today's prices;
1960–70 – multiply by 20 to equate to today's prices;
1970–74 – multiply by 16 to equate to today's prices;
1975–77 – multiply by 11 to equate to today's prices;
1978–80 – multiply by 7 to equate to today's prices;

1980–87 – multiply by 4 to equate to today's prices;
1987–91 – multiply by 2 to equate to today's prices;
1991–97 – multiply by 1.5 to equate to today's prices.

Since 1997, the rate of inflation, by the standards of most of the 20th century, has been very low, averaging less than the Labour government's originally stated aim of 2.5 per cent (since reduced to 2 per cent). You don't need me to tell you that some things, such as telephone charges and many items made in the Far East (notably China), are going down in price; while others, such as houses, have moved up very sharply.

> *I've been rich and I've been poor.*
> *Rich is better.*
>
> **Sophie Tucker**

Amazonia

In spring 1996, not so long ago, James Marcus flew to Seattle to be interviewed for a job with Amazon. In his words: 'Amazon had opened its (virtual) doors the previous July, and while business had picked up impressively it hadn't been so long since a bell had rung in the office each time somebody made a purchase ... The web was still mostly the province of geeks, technicians, New Age nuts, scientists, and academics of the racier sort who had been nudged online by their institutional overseers.'

Marcus was hired, and though he asked for a salary of $50,000 he agreed to work for $44,000 and the option to buy 1,000 shares at $1 each. His contract said, *inter alia*: 'The Employee acknowledges that he has been informed of the nature of the Company's business activities and recognizes that his position may involve a high degree of job-related stress. As a condition of his employment, the Employee agrees that he will not bring an action against the Company for the recovery of any damages alleged to have resulted from such job-related stress, and will indemnify the Company and hold the Company harmless against any such claims by any of the Employee's relatives or by other third parties.'

Marcus was employee number 55. Within two years there were 8,000, and by that time Jeff Bezos had taken Amazon public. What happened to Marcus and his options? Because Bezos had raised more money, Marcus had more options — a few thousand — and he also borrowed some money and bought some shares. But he still had no cash: 'My finances had gotten even shakier. Persistent illness sent my wife to the hospital on two different occasions, and Amazon's rather skimpy insurance

1

package covered only a fraction of the costs. Each time, I found myself in the business office at the hospital, cobbling together instalment agreements that could easily take me years to pay off. The account managers, young guys who positively radiated good health, were so reasonable I felt like crying. I kept shaking their hands. I couldn't stop thanking them.'

Then Marcus decided to sell a few shares, and received $53,913. As he said: 'This permanently changed my relationship for better or worse.'

Then came the real dotcom boom. The Amazon share price climbed and climbed almost without pause, and on 15 December 1998 an analyst set a target of $400 a share. On that day alone the stock rose to $46, and soon passed $400. At the peak, Marcus's options were worth no less than $9 million.

It couldn't last and it didn't. On 10 March 1999, the NASDAQ index of high-tech stocks peaked at 5,048. It then slumped and Amazon slumped with it. Marcus's options lost more than 95 per cent of their value.

--------- **Buying houses** ---------

The average home in Britain now costs more than £200,000. In 1950 it was less than £5,000.

Buying and selling houses has been a very profitable exercise for the last 50 years. A combination of rising prosperity, inflation, tax relief on mortgage interest payments and, above all, the method of financing the purchase of houses whereby banks and building societies will lend a multiple of the ever-rising income of most people, have all meant that, over the medium term, house prices have risen far faster than the rate of inflation.

House prices in Britain rose steadily during the 1950s and 60s, but took off in the early 1970s as the economy boomed, interest rates remained low and liquidity was pumped into the economy by a Conservative government attempting to revitalise business activity. House prices rose 37.4 per cent in 1972 and a further 32.1 per cent in 1973. The government took fright and raised interest rates from 8.5 to 11 per cent, and the market cooled sharply. I remember we turned down an offer of £42,000 for our house in 1973 (we had paid £9,000 for it in 1967 but we had doubled its size for an extra £4,000 in 1970 – don't these sums seem laughable in 2006?), and were happy to accept £29,500, i.e. a drop of 30 per cent, for it eighteen months later in early 1975.

> *A little house well filled, a field well-tilled, and a little wife well willed, are great riches.*
>
> **Benjamin Franklin**

As with many other items, the prices of houses in the 1930s are hard to believe today – mind you, so are the wages and salaries most people received. Newly built houses in Edgware, north London, were being advertised as 'The Little Mansions of Edgware' and could be bought for £775 cash or £25 down and 25s 6d a week. Richard Costain was building houses on the Greenford Estate in west London with three bedrooms, two living rooms, bath, kitchen and car space, and selling them for £730.

Even in the recession of the mid-1970s, house prices in general didn't fall in absolute terms because retail inflation was so bad – it reached 25 per cent in 1975 – but they fell in relative terms. As a result there was virtually none of the negative equity which plagued the market in the early 1990s. Home-owners were baled out of their mortgage debts by inflation.

How important is the housing market?

Very, because of the high percentage of the population who own their own homes, most of them borrowing very large sums to do so. In 1900 about 10 per cent owned their own homes. In 1950 it was still only 30 per cent. Now it's 70 per cent. This makes the level of interest rates very important to most people. When rates are raised 1 per cent from, say, 4 to 5 per cent, it doesn't sound very much. However, if you're borrowing £200,000 it's an *extra* £2,000 a year or £167 a month in mortgage interest payments. When you consider that interest rates in the early 1990s went up to 12 per cent, it's easy to understand the mayhem that was caused. Compared with 4 per cent on a loan of £200,000, 12 per cent meant an *extra* £16,000 a year or £1,333 a month.

> **Live within your income even if you have to borrow money to do so.**
>
> **Josh Billings**

The British system of lending for house purchase is a guaranteed mechanism for house price rises. Further-more, as the lending is geared to income, it means that prices will rise faster than the rate of inflation because most sections of society, especially those that can afford houses, have become adept at making sure that their incomes rise faster than the rate of inflation.

The average price of a house has remained consistently around three to three-and-a-half times earnings since the mid-1950s. Only in the late 1950s and early 1980s did it fall just below three times, and only in the early 1970s and in the last few years has it risen above four times.

The growth in the value of the average home in Britain since the second quarter of 1968 is no less than 4,300 per cent, with the highest ever quarterly increase in prices – 50 per cent – in the first quarter of 1973. Furthermore, there is no Capital Gains Tax on owner-occupied properties, whereas on other assets there is now a rate of 40 per cent. Nevertheless, timing has been quite important. There have been times, usually prompted by a sharp rise in interest rates, when house prices have fallen.

—— Are there jewels in the grave? ——

The first *Sunday Times* Rich List compiled in 1989 showed that nearly 25 per cent of the 200 people listed were hereditary landowners. Between them, the 95 richest landowners owned 2.3 million acres, or 3.85 per cent of Britain.

This was all different from 60 years ago when, in 1947, the 7th Earl Spencer was so hard up that he was forced to ransack the graves of his ancestors in search of jewels. The Earl, whose granddaughter married Prince Charles and whose grandson had to fight off an £8 million settlement bid from his estranged wife in 1997 (by which time his wealth was calculated at £80 million), didn't find any jewels, but he stripped the lead from the coffins to repair the roof of his country house at Althorp.

> *Nobody talks more of free enterprise and competition and of the best man winning than the man who inherited his father's store or farm.*
>
> **C. Wright Mills**

In the 1870s, the first Duke of Westminster's annual income was £295–325,000 (£33–36 million in today's money), the Duke of Portland's was £190–200,000 (£21–22 million) and the Duke of Bedford's £250–285,000 (£25–28 million).

By the 1880s, eighteen aristocrats had incomes of £100,000 (£11 million) or more and 78 had more than £50,000 (£5.5 million). By contrast, only eleven businessmen created fortunes of over £2 million (£220 million) between 1809 and 1879. However, the following 60 years produced 83.

Just 7,000 people owned 80 per cent of the land in Britain.

> *My formula for success is rise early, work late and strike oil.*
>
> **J. Paul Getty**

Negative equity

The phrase was unknown before 1990. At that point many people learnt its meaning quickly and painfully. This is what happened.

The world economy grew very fast from 1982 to 1987, fed by a big drop in the price of oil and by business- and consumer-friendly policies by some of the world governments, notably in the USA and the UK. Further- more, this growth was fuelled by easy money, with loans at low interest rates readily available to both commercial and private borrowers.

Because for most people a very high percentage of the purchase price is borrowed, house prices rise sharply when interest rates are low, and stagnate or – perish the thought – even fall when they are high. At dinner parties in the late 1980s, and again in the early years of this century, people were congratulating each other on how clever they were because their house was 'worth' twice what it was just two or three years ago.

In Britain house prices rose sharply, and financing the purchase had become very easy, with 90, 95, even 100 per cent loans available. On a £100,000 mortgage, 10 per cent was £833, quite lot but manageable if both partners were earning £1,500 a month. The sums looked different by the end of 1989, when interest rates had been raised to 15 per cent and some lenders were charging 18 to 20 per cent. Now the monthly repayment was £1,600 a month and, as the government-planned slowdown hit, one of the partners was made redundant.

> *I can do Addition, she said, if you give me time – but I can't do Subtraction, under any circumstances.*
>
> **Lewis Carroll,**
> ***Through the Looking-Glass***

The downward spiral was established. The couple needed to sell, but so did lots of others. The house that had been bought for £110,000 with a £100,000 mortgage couldn't be sold — certainly not for £110,000 and indeed not for £100,000, nor £90,000 nor even £80,000. You could probably give it away for £70,000, but then you'd owe the mortgage company £30,000, and you've just sold the collateral.

Ah, so that's what negative equity means.

They did have Prime Minister John Major's reassuring phrase to console themselves:

IF it ISN'T HURTING it ISN'T WORKING

What is rich?

Certainly being a millionaire, whether in pounds, euros or dollars, doesn't make you rich. The rapid rise in house prices in the developed world means that there are millions of millionaires. Even having cash or investable assets up to £500,000 or $1 million doesn't make you rich, merely one of the 'mass-affluent', as the financial advisory world would describe you. Above, say, £5 million or $10 million will bring you real security and a lot of worries about kidnappers and demotivation of your children.

And being rich brings different benefits and hazards in different countries. The egalitarian Swedes don't think anyone should be seriously rich, so their punitive – some would say confiscatory – taxes drive people like the Rausings (one of the richest families in the country) to Britain and Björn Borg to Monaco. In Brazil the rich are frightened of what the masses of poor people might do to them, and either drive around in armoured cars or fly around in helicopters.

> *Every morning I get up and look through the Forbes list of the richest people in America. If I'm not there I go to work.*
>
> **Robert Orben**

As for 'What is rich?', you have to make more effort to be recognised. Ten years ago, you had to have assets of only about £80 million to get into the top 200 richest people in Britain. Now it's over £200 million. To get into the top 100 then you needed just over £100 million, now it's over £400 million; as for the exclusive club of the top 50, in 1995 it was £200 million; now it's over £700 million.

Cars – for the elite or the masses?

Nothing has quite captured the imagination of people throughout the world like the motor car. It has brought freedom, mobility and the chance to express individuality.

As with all such inventions, the price has come down (in relative terms) and the quality has gone up.

In 1920, William Morris, later Lord Nuffield, sold 2,000 of his very popular Morris Oxfords for £400 each (£22,000 in today's money). As the immediate post-war boom turned to recession, he cut the price to £225 (£12,375) and sold 3,000 the following year.

His price-cutting wasn't as fierce as Henry Ford's in the USA. In 1907 he had said: 'I will build a motor car for the great multitude. It will be large enough for the family but small enough for the individual to run and care for. It will be constructed of the best materials, by the best men to be hired, after the simplest designs that modern engineering can devise. But it will be so low in price that no man making a good salary will be unable to own one.' He was true to his word. His Model T, known as 'tin lizzies', began life at $950, but by 1926 they were only $290.

At the top end of the scale, when Henry Royce signed his agreement with the Hon. C.S. Rolls in 1904 to buy chassis from him, there were four types:

a 10hp two-cylinder model to sell at £395 (£43,500 in today's money);

a 15hp three-cylinder model to sell at £500 (£55,000);

a 20hp four-cylinder model to sell at £650 (£75,500);

a 30hp six-cylinder model to sell at £890 (£98,000).

While Royce was turning out these cars in the first years of the 20th century, he was paying his key men 5 shillings (25p or £27.50) a week. For this they were working 100 hours a week.

Whoever said money can't buy happiness simply didn't know how to go shopping.

At the same time, a 60hp Mercedes cost £2,500 (£275,000) and a six-cylinder Napier, perhaps Rolls-Royce's most formidable early competitor, £1,050 (£115,500).

When Rolls-Royce was floated in 1908 and shares offered to the public, the prospectus showed Royce's salary as chief engineer and works director as £1,250 (£137,500) plus 4 per cent of profits over £10,000 (£1,100,000). Rolls, as technical managing director, received £750 (£82,500) and also the 4 per cent.

Britain came relatively late to motoring, handing an initial advantage to the French and Germans. Siegfried Marcus had produced a petrol-engined car in Vienna in 1865, and by 1888 Karl Benz was selling his cars in Germany and France. In the 1890s, the French companies De Dion and Panhard et Levassor were pressing ahead with manufacture. However, in Britain development was held back by laws designed to protect a former way of life (riding horses and travelling in carriages) and, thanks to a powerful lobby in both Houses of Parliament, the interests of the railway companies.

The 1865 Locomotive Act stated, *inter alia*, that at least three persons had to be employed to drive a self-propelled vehicle while the vehicle was in motion; one of the passengers was required to precede the vehicle on foot by at least twenty yards; drivers had to give way to all other traffic, which was empowered to stop self-propelled vehicles just by raising a hand; the speed limit was 4 mph, or 2 mph in towns and villages; and there was a licence fee of £10 (about £110 today) *per county* in which the vehicle was used.

By the 1950s, the Bentley Mark VI was the fastest four-seater saloon in world and, at £6,000 (£180,000) for overseas buyers, the most expensive. The Rolls-Royce Silver Cloud in 1955 was £4,796 10s 1d (£120,000) – don't you love the 1d, the equivalent of 0.4 of a p?

By comparison, the Jaguar 3.4 S-type was £1,669 (£33,500), the 3.8 S-type was £1,759 (£35,000), the Mark X was £2,022 (£40,000) and the Rover 3-litre was £1,641 (£32,500). By the early 1970s, the Rolls-Royce Silver Shadow had moved up to £10,400 (£180,000) and the Corniche was £14,000 (£250,000) but changing hands at £17–18,000 (£300–320,000). In 1984, the Bentley Eight launched at £50,000 (£200,000).

If the automobile had followed the same development cycle as the computer, a Rolls-Royce would today cost $100, get a million miles per gallon, and explode once a year, killing everyone inside.

Robert Cringely

And if people think about the price of cars, they think a lot more about the price of petrol. At 90p a litre (or £4 a gallon), people think it's very expensive. In real terms, it was more expensive in 1950 when it was 3 shillings a gallon (15p, but £4.50 at today's prices). And in the 1950s, especially in 1956–7, the time of the Suez Crisis, it got worse. In 1957, a gallon cost 6 shillings and 1½ pence (30.5p, but £7.50 in today's money).

The most entertaining men around

The young heiress Isabel de Rosnay (daughter of Sir James Goldsmith) told the *Daily Express*: 'When I was 17 one could never be sure whether one was meeting a fortune-hunter or not. There were always three basic clues – they were good-looking and amusing and their backgrounds were never very clear. But oh, they are such good company. They are the most entertaining men around.'

> *Money is just the poor man's credit card.*
>
> **Marshall McLuhan**

The company car

Before the 1970s, company cars were the preserve of the owners of a business, the directors of large public companies and those who *needed* them to do their job, i.e. reps.

13

During the 1970s, in a futile attempt to combat inflation, governments introduced incomes policies which put a cap on salaries or, at times of real crisis, imposed a freeze. However, accountants are notoriously clever at finding ways around government taxes or impositions, and the 'company car' came into its own as a way of increasing a good employee's salary.

Once established, the envy syndrome set in and the company-car habit exploded, so that by the end of the century about 2.5 million of the 26 million cars on the road were company cars.

This was in spite of the fact that the envy of those excluded from this privilege had forced governments to raise taxes on this 'benefit in kind' to a level which negated all the advantages. The company car remains popular because it's seen as a status symbol and the costs are somehow hidden. And the fact that all the partners in accountancy firms still have them suggests that the government hasn't fully killed all the benefits.

—— **When in doubt, turn to sex** ——

David Sullivan, founder of the *Sunday Sport* and owner of the Private Shops chain, began his business career as an advertising account executive handling dog food. That was the day job. The night job was selling nude pictures by mail order through Exchange and Mart. He recalls: 'I offered twenty nude lovelies for £1. I went from earning £88 a month to £800 a week and I only had to work three hours a day.'

During the 1970s he ran 125 sex shops and 25 magazines, and in 1982 he founded the *Sunday Sport* with the emphasis on semi-naked women. By 1990, he was reckoned to be Britain's 134th-richest individual, with a fortune of £60 million. By 2005, the Rich List had moved him up to 82nd, with £550 million. He still hasn't got past that other entrepreneur who understands his fellow man's need for titillation, Paul Raymond, who has £50 million more and is rated at 76th equal.

Raymond's Revuebar was a leader of full nudity and G-string shows back in the 1960s. In 2004 it re-opened as a gay club called Too 2 Much. Raymond still owns the freehold.

—— £15 a week? No, £15 a year! ——

Almost non-existent today (and almost certainly consisting of immigrants, legal or otherwise), domestic servants both male and female, but especially female, formed a significant part of the workforce in the Victorian era. The 1891 Census showed that nearly 16 per cent of workers were deemed to be in 'Domestic Service'.

What were they paid?

According to advertisements in *The Times* between 1850 and 1870, the pay of cooks rose from £15 to £19 – a week? No. A month then? No. Not a year? Yes. In today's money, it's a rise from £1,650 to £2,090. For housemaids it rose from £11 to £14 (£1,120 to £1,540).

This might not seem much, but it was attractive compared with industrial wages. The factory reports in the 1870s of the giant textiles manufacturer, Courtaulds, are full of complaints about the difficulty of preventing girls going into service.

The demand for nursemaids obviously increased, because their wages grew from £11 to £17.

Agricultural labourers in England in 1830s were earning 12–14 shillings a week (60–70p, or £66–77 in today's money, just £3,400–4,000 a year).

———— Cockle the field! ————

In gambling, money is everything and the odds are important. So that you don't get lost, here are the slang terms for the odds:

Odds	Slang
Evens	Levels, Scotch
2/1	Bottle
3/1	Carpet, Gimmel
4/1	Rouf
5/1	Hand
5/2	Face
6/1	Xs
7/1	Nevs
8/1	T.H.
9/1	Enin
10/1	Cockle Net
11/10	Tips
33/1	Double Carpet
100/30	Burlington Bertie

And, in everyday life, I'm sure you know that a quid is £1 but did you know that a Nugget or a Dollar are also £1, a Jack, Blue or Godiva is £5, a Tenner, Pavarotti or Cock is £10, a Score is £20, a Pony is £25, a Bull's Eye is £50, a Ton or Century is £100, a Monkey is £500, a Grand or Rio is £1,000 and, finally, an Archer is £2,000?

This last, of course, refers to Jeffrey Archer's offer of £2,000 to the prostitute Monica Coghlan.

——— What's a whitesmith or ——— a japanner?

A survey of jobs and careers in mid-Victorian Britain is interesting not only for the jobs involved, some of them now extinct, but also for what it shows about the financial rewards.

At the top on 35 shillings a week (£1.75, or £192 in today's money) were:

3,150 scientific, surgical and optical instrument-makers
1,150 scale-makers
2,200 leather case-makers
15,400 watch-makers
11,000 jewellery-makers
9,300 engine drivers

Below them on 28–30 shillings (£1.40–1.50, or £154–165 in today's money) were:

28,350 printers and binders
9,000 hat-makers
13,600 ivory, bone and woodworkers
20,300 earthenware workers
44,250 arms- and tool-makers
91,700 ironworkers
39,000 cabinet-makers and upholsterers
2,200 musical instrument-makers
7,000 bakers' and butchers' men

Anyone who lives within their means suffers from a lack of imagination.

Oscar Wilde

On a mere 25 shillings (£1.25, or £137.50 in today's money) were:

100,000 seamen
30,000 coach- and harness-makers
19,200 tanners, curriers and skinners
130,000 blacksmiths, whitesmiths (people who polished metal as opposed to forging it) and hardware workers

6,700 laceworkers
11,000 straw, rush, bark and caneworkers
8,500 oilmen, polishers and japanners (people who
varnished to give hard gloss)
50,000 workers in copper, brass, tin, zinc, lead and other
metals

Next, on 21–23 shillings (£1.05–1.15, or £115–126 in today's money) were:

64,500 railway workmen
11,500 postmen
81,700 coachmen, cabmen and carriers
233,500 miners
143,000 cotton, calico and fustian workers
4,300 chimney sweeps
98,600 servants

Further down, on 15–20 shillings (75p–£1, or £82.50 –110 in today's money) were:

19,500 sailors
50,000 fishermen
14,500 policemen
6,200 coastguards and militiamen
2,100 civil service messengers
25,000 maltsters and brewers
2,700 glove-makers
1,820 straw workers
29,500 dock labourers
44,000 horsekeepers, drovers and gamekeepers

And, at the bottom, on 14 shillings (70p, or £77 in today's money):

880,000 farm labourers
258,000 labourers
10,500 road labourers and scavengers

In mid-Victorian Britain, the Irish were worse off than the Scottish, with an average annual income per head of £14 (£1,540 today) against £23 10s (£2,585). These paled into significance against England and Wales's £32 (£3,520).

The stationmaster at St Pancras, one of London's leading railway stations, was paid £265 (£29,000) a year. That would allow him only two servants to look after his family.

The sheer number of women and girls in domestic service of one sort or another is staggering. In 1881, no fewer than 1,170,000 women over fifteen were domestic servants. They were joined by a further 99,000 girls under fifteen and another 276,000 described as washer-women or charwomen. This total was no less than 12 per cent of the female population.

> *The meek may inherit the earth – but not its mineral rights.*
>
> **J. Paul Getty**

———— Hang the director ————

Having said that there was virtually no inflation in Britain before the 20th century, there were in fact occasional bouts of quite severe inflation, most notably in Tudor times under Henry VIII and during the Napoleonic Wars.

The cost of living virtually doubled between 1797 and 1812. This was partly due to the war with France (wars are always inflationary) and partly to mistakes by the Bank of England which showed signs of laxness in its lending policies. Furthermore, it had begun to issue banknotes, leading to many forgeries which, in turn, led to many hangings and transportations of forgers. William Cobbett wrote in his Political Register: 'This villainous Bank has slaughtered more people than would people a State. With the rope, the prison, the hulk and the transport ship, this Bank has destroyed, perhaps, fifty thousand persons, including the widows and orphans of the victims.'

One correspondent wrote to the *Examiner* and suggested that all hangings for forgery should be carried out by a Director of the Bank. Leigh Hunt, the editor, wrote: 'Our correspondent professes to have been some time debating with himself, whether it would not be still more effective if the Forger were to hang the Director.'

If God had only given me a clear sign; like making a large deposit in my name at a Swiss bank.

Woody Allen

The really poor

Peter Wilsher shows us in his book, *The Pound in Your Pocket 1870–1970*, what could happen if, at the height of the strength of the British Empire, you were a member of the honest working class and were unlucky enough to fall ill: 'On 1 January 1870 – when few people either in England or abroad would have questioned Bagehot's description of the City of London as "by far the greatest combination of economical power and economical delicacy that the world has ever known" – an inquest was opened by the Coroner of St Mary-Le-Bone into the death of an elderly woman who had died from lack of food. Her husband, a cab-driver, was referred to as an honest, hardworking man, who had always maintained his home in good order.'

'Unfortunately, six weeks before, his cab had been involved in an accident and he had been taken to hospital with fairly extensive injuries. This meant that his livelihood ceased and there was no income or savings on which his wife could call. Accordingly, she applied for relief from the Parish, and, after a delay of two weeks, she was duly granted assistance – to the hardly generous extent of 2s 6d, plus one loaf of bread, then costing 7d a quartern, per week.'

'On his release from hospital the husband, being without work or money, also applied for relief. After some further delay he was granted no cash, but an additional half a loaf per week. Despite further application no more could be prised out of the authorities. This was partly because the Relief Officer had forgotten, or omitted, to note the fact that there were now two people dependent on his help instead of one. Not unnaturally the wife fell

22

seriously ill on the meagre sustenance available, and although the doctor was eventually called and prescribed beef tea and wine (though without specifying where these were to come from) it was too late, and she shortly expired. In evidence the husband stated that with the 2s 6d his wife had bought tea (of which the normal working-class quality then cost 3s 4d a lb), sugar (at around 9d a lb) butter (very expensive, at up to 2s a lb) and a few other necessities. He also mentioned the rent they paid was 2s a week.'

'The jury, it was hardly surprising to hear, were deeply incensed by the case and strongly in favour of impeaching the Relief Officer for neglect. This was, with some difficulty, overruled by the Coroner.'

Meanwhile, over in the City of London ...

> **I'd like to live as a poor man, but with lots of money.**
>
> **Pablo Picasso**

Money by weight

This is what a Swiss industrialist found when he went to cash a cheque in a City of London bank in the 1870s: 'When I returned to the bank a little before nine o'clock I was shown to a seat facing a counter where five cashiers conducted their business. At five minutes to nine the official to whom I had to give my cheque took his place behind the counter. I had it in my hand and showed it to him. He did not say a word but emptied several little bags of gold coins into a drawer. Then he produced the well-known little cash shovel that is used for coins in banks. And then he just waited. At the stroke of nine he asked me if I wanted gold or banknotes. I said I wanted gold. He did not count any of the sovereigns or half sovereigns but simply weighed them on his scales and then put them on the counter without taking any further notice of me.'

Gordon Bennett

No wonder people say 'Gordon Bennett!' when they are amazed. James Gordon Bennett (1841–1918), was earning over $1 million a year (c. $20 million today) by the time he was 25. He lived most of his life in France and conducted the running of his newspaper, the *New York Herald*, by cable. He financed Stanley's expedition to Africa to find Livingstone, and married for the first time – at the age of 73 – Baroness de Reuter of Reuters fame. Flamboyant in the extreme, he bought a restaurant in Monte Carlo so that he could move someone sitting at his favourite table, and then gave the restaurant as a tip to the waiter.

Glad you live now and not 200 years ago?

'The summer of 1800 had brought a fearful drought which destroyed potatoes and other root crops. The harvesting of grain began early, but rainstorms then set in with such strength and persistency that work had to be abandoned and the crops left to rot in the fields. Severe shortages and high bread prices were the result. All over the country, horses were slaughtered for meat or left to starve, cottagers killed their pigs, and many were reduced to eating turnips and nettles. In the capital, crowds of 'poor women, without cloaks or bonnets, some with scarcely cloaths to cover them', gathered to demand cheaper bread. In Nottingham, a desperate scramble for flour ensued. Mobs railed against millers, grain barges were plundered, and knots of hungry women hurled stones at the premises of bakers. They then joined their menfolk in ambushing a detachment of yeomanry carrying a cartload of grain. Several cotton mills were also attacked on the grounds that they had caused the hardship which left most of the population too poor to buy the essentials of life.'

From *The Real Oliver Twist* by John Waller

> *I've got all the money I need if I die by four o'clock this afternoon.*
>
> **Henry Youngman**

—— Funerals – the Victorians —— loved them

Funerals were taken more seriously by the Victorians than they are today. In 1870 London, it cost £5 9s or £5.45 (£600 today) to bury an adult, and £2 2s or £2.10 (£230) to bury a child. However, people didn't stop there. Add in flowers, headstone, funeral cloaks, hatbands, scarves, gilded hearses and mourners' coaches, and an unskilled labourer's family could be spending £40–50 (£4,500–5,000). As he would have been earning £60 a year, his family were spending about 75 per cent of his annual wage.

> **Money is something you have to make in case you don't die.**
>
> **Max Ashas**

You are what you eat

By contrast, in 1900 when Great Britain's empire was at its peak, the reality of life for at least a third of the population was an existence of grinding poverty. Seebohm Rowntree wrote *Poverty: A Study of Town Life* and Charles Booth wrote *Life and Labours of the People of London*, and pricked the consciences of the comfortable of the Edwardian era.

They revealed the weekly expenditure on food per head of the different classes:

Lower working class   1s 6d–3s
    (7.5–15p or £7.50–15.00 in today's money)
Upper working class   3–4s
    (15–20p or £15–20)
Lower middle class   5–10s
    (25–50p or £25–50)
Middle class   10–15s
    (50–75p or £50–75)
Upper Middle class   20–30s
    (£1–1.50 or £100–150)

A pint of beer cost two old pence a pint (0.83 of today's penny, or 92p today) so beer is one thing that's

26

gone up more than twice the rate of inflation. There's more tax, of course, but maybe it's time for another look at the brewing and pub businesses by the monopolies commission.

———— New York for £3.50 ————

As we move into the 20th century, how is everyone faring?

Ernest Bevin, who served in Churchill's wartime Cabinet and became arguably one of Britain's best-ever Foreign Secretaries in Attlee's Labour administration from 1945–50, switched his job in 1896 as a bakehouse boy on 6 shillings a week (30p or £33 today) – and his working week was twelve hours a day, six days a week – to become a mineral-water wagon minder for 10 shillings (50p or £55). By contrast, in that year the Conservative Prime Minister, Lord Salisbury, was living on his landed estate estimated to be worth £6 million (£660 million today), and the former Liberal leader, William Gladstone, had retired to his 7,000-acre estate with its 2,500 tenants paying rents totalling £10–12,000 (over £1 million in today's money).

Mind you, £1 in 1896 bought quite a lot. You could have 80 two-pound jars of fruit jam or six bottles of whisky or 1,440 herrings at six for 1d or 30 gallons of fresh milk or the rent of a shop and house for nearly a month or fifteen pairs of ladies' shoes. If you had £3 10s, you could sail to New York.

And some people received plenty of those pounds. In 1896, the Archbishop of Canterbury was receiving an extremely heavenly £15,000 (£1.65 million in today's

27

money) a year. By the end of the 20th century, the Archbishop's stipend was just over £50,000. In other words, his income had gone up by just over three times, while the cost of living had increased by over 100 times. Lord Overton, the owner of the Showfield Chemical Works in Glasgow, gave £10,000 (£1.1 million) to charity in 1896, while paying his workers 3d an hour for a twelve-hour day, seven days a week, and fining them a day's wages if they took Sunday off.

There were plenty of bargains. A Kodak camera complete with film for twelve photographs cost £1 1s (£115 today). You could go to the battlefields of Waterloo for £1.

> *A bargain is something you can't use at a price you can't resist.*
>
> **Franklin Jones**

The one thing that was expensive was riding – indeed anything to do with a horse – especially in fashionable Rotten Row in Hyde Park in London. According to Peter Wilsher: 'As *Women's Life* said in an article on "The Cost of Riding in Rotten Row": "Riding under the cheapest conditions is an expensive luxury; but in Rotten Row it becomes even more so, as you see there only the finest 'cattle.'" The "cattle" ran out at anything between £100 (considered "cheap for a saddle-horse") and 250 guineas, for thoroughbred with a pedigree. As such animals were only ridden during the Season, and never for more than two or three years, the minimum cost of horse-flesh alone was £30 a year, which was raised to £150 a year, after adding in shoeing, harnessing, forage and the services of the "vet", and probably to £200, after investing in at least three smart riding habits at £5 each, and the groom (a necessity) whose annual licence fee was 15s and whose wages came to at least 25s a week. And that only covered one person's recreational riding – a well-appointed, one-horse brougham cost at least £150 a year to keep on the road, with coachman's wages at anything between 25s and 50s a week, and a crack carriage and pair (with "indispensable" footman at another guinea) something in the region of £315. Naturally, this did not include anything for initial investment in the motive power of the horse or in the vehicle itself. "The carriage horse is a costly animal – one of 17 hands would be valued at quite 159 guineas, and as at least three are wanted, one being kept in reserve, a large cheque is required in this direction." No wonder there was a substantial trade in hiring out such equipment. A carriage and pair, complete with coachman, could be rented from stables in most towns at a figure in the region of £250 a year. But even that can hardly have appeared cheap at the time when at least five million manual workers in the country (including some of the soldiers, sailors, policemen, farm labourers and domestic servants) were subsisting with their families on something under one-fifth of this sum.'

———— Money or your life ————

They say – and I hope I'm never put to the test – that when people are told to abandon an aircraft in an emergency, they still spend time scrabbling in the overhead lockers for their duty-free purchases. Certainly when the

Titanic went down in April 1912, Mrs Dickinson Bishop decided not to waste time retrieving her jewellery from the safe, thereby abandoning $11,000 (over $1 million today). Major Arthur Penchen left a tin box with over $300,000 (over $30 million) in stocks and shares.

Shopping

Selfridges in Oxford Street opened in 1909 amid much fanfare. Ten people claimed the distinction of being the first to buy, among them a Madame Barry of Bond Street who bought a handkerchief for 1s 4d (6.5p or £7 today). I hope it was silk! Another claimant bought a morning coat and waistcoat for £3 10s (£3.50 or £385).

Outside, Claridges and the Savoy were charging 7s 6d (37.5p or £41) for a single room, and beer was a penny a pint (0.4p or 45p) in the public bar or double that in the saloon bar. Public school fees were £38 a year (£4,180). At the top schools now they are £25,000. A 75-day cruise of the West Indies could be had for £75 (£8,250).

In 1914, a worker in engineering was earning 22s 10d a week (£1.14 or £125 in today's money); a pint of beer cost 2½d (1p or £1.10); a front-row seat at the Royal Opera House, Covent Garden, cost 1 guinea (£1.05 or £115); dinner at the Savoy was 7s 6d (37.5p or £40), and a double room there cost £1 5s (£1.25 or £137).

A whole evening for two at the Royal Opera House followed by dinner and a night at the Savoy was £4. It sounds cheap, though in today's money it was £440, and it was equal to a whole month's earnings for a worker in the engineering industry. Not too many of them at the Royal Opera or the Savoy in those days, then!

—— God bless that Lord George! ——

In 1908, pensions of between 1 shilling (50p or £5.50) and 5 shillings (25p or £27.50) a week became payable as of right to persons over 70, 'subject to a means test but without the stigma of Poor Relief'.

Flora Thompson, in her book *Lark Rise*, described what it meant to many: 'When the Old Age Pensions began, life was transformed for some aged cottagers. They were suddenly rich. Independent for life! At first when they went to the Post Office to draw it, tears of gratitude would run down the cheeks of some, and they would say as they picked up their money, "God bless that Lord George!" (for they could not believe one so power-ful and munificent could be a plain "Mr") and "God bless you, miss!", and there were flowers from their gardens, and apples from their trees for the girl who merely handed over the money.'

—— **Damn nincompoop bankers!** ——

At the end of the First World War – the most deadly in history – the Allies, especially Britain and France, were determined to force Germany not only to admit her guilt for starting the war but also to pay heavy reparations. The British demanded £24 billion and the French £44 billion (£1,300 billion and over £2,400 billion in today's money).

The great economist John Maynard Keynes, in charge of preparing the British Treasury position, said: 'That's ridiculous, damn nincompoop bankers! The Allies will be lucky to get £2 billion.'

He said of Woodrow Wilson, the US President: 'He's a blind and deaf Don Quixote'; and of Lloyd George, the British Prime Minster: 'He's a hostage to his parliamentary majority and public opinion'; and of Georges Clemenceau, President of France: 'He wants to crush Germany for a generation.'

Of Germany's capacity to pay, he said: 'Her only means of paying was through an export surplus. Pre-war her deficit had been £74 million. By reducing imports and increasing exports, she might turn this into a £50 million surplus. Spread over 30 years this would come to a capital sum of £1,700 million invested at 6 per cent. Add £100–200 million for transfers of gold, property etc. and £2 billion is a safe maximum figure of Germany's capacity to pay.'

He took a pessimistic view of Germany's attitude if punishing reparations were imposed: 'Vengeance, I dare predict, will not be limp. Nothing can delay for long that final civil war between the forces of reaction and the despairing convulsions of revolution, before which the horrors of the late German war will fade into nothing and will destroy, whoever is the victor, the civilisation and progress of our generation.'

That was a pretty accurate forecast. He was joined in his accuracy by Marshal Foch, the leader of the French forces, who, when he read the details of the Treaty of Versailles in 1919, said: 'This is merely a twenty-year truce.' Accurate to the year!

Keynes resigned from the Treasury and wrote *The Economic Consequences of the Peace*. This was universally acclaimed by economists. Others were not so sure. Neville Chamberlain said: 'It weakened British and French resistance to Hitler because they agreed with him that the Versailles Treaty was unfair.'

It gave America an argument for abandoning Europe to its fate. And, of course, it gave Hitler the excuse to break the Treaty.

Buy British

This is what Maynard Keynes said on the BBC in January 1931: 'The best guess I can make is that whenever you save five shillings, you put a man out of work for a day. Your saving that five shillings adds to unemployment to the extent of one man for one day and so on in proportion. On the other hand, whenever you buy goods you increase employment – though they must be British, home-produced goods if you are to increase employment in this country ... Therefore, oh patriotic housewives of Britain, sally out tomorrow early into the streets and go to the wonderful sales that are everywhere advertised.

You will do yourselves good – for never were things so cheap, cheap beyond your dreams. Lay in stock of household linen, sheets and blankets to supply all your needs. And have the added joy that you are increasing employment, adding to the wealth of your country, because you are setting on foot useful activities, bringing a chance and hope to Lancashire, Yorkshire and Belfast.'

He was right about the bargains. A spring tweed coat was £1 (£50 in today's money) and Whiteley's department store had reduced men's mackintoshes from 14s 6d (72.5p or £36) to 10s (£25).

For producers it wasn't so good. Wheat in Liverpool had fallen to 5s 9d a quarter, a price not seen since the reign of Charles II. It had been 12s 2d in 1925 and 46s 11d back in 1870.

—— Work for only fifteen hours —— a week?

Keynes predicted in the 1930s that in a hundred years' time, people in Britain would be eight times better off (arguably that target has been reached already) and that the long struggle to earn enough money to meet basic needs would be over. He thought that the majority of people would then work for only fifteen hours or so a week. He thought that a few would work harder in the pursuit of wealth but the majority would not, seeing the love of money 'as one of those semi-criminal, semi-pathological propensities'.

Clearly, he was wrong. He underestimated people's desires for more than just the satisfaction of their basic needs.

Income tax at 2d

How did people, rich and poor, cope with income tax?

Income tax was first introduced in 1799, primarily to finance the war against Napoleon. It was levied on incomes above £60 (£6,600 today). It was discontinued after Napoleon's defeat in 1815 but reintroduced in 1842 at 7d (2.92p) in the £. It was gradually reduced to its lowest level of 2d in 1875.

Although Gladstone reduced income tax to 4d (1.67p) in the £ in 1866 and Prime Minister Northcote halved it in the 1870s, there was at that time a wealth tax. Owners of houses worth £20-plus had to pay tax under schedule A, at the rate of just over 1 per cent. In 1874, tax on a house worth £20 was 4s 9d. If applied today, the tax on a house valued at £300,000 would be £3,570.

Thereafter the standard rate of income tax rose steadily, reaching 1 shilling (5p) in the £ in 1900. In his 1911 Budget, Lloyd George raised it to 1s 2d, with 1s 8d for the higher rate. During the First World War it rose sharply to 6 shillings (30p). It dropped back during the

1920s to 4 shillings (20p), before rising again to 5 shillings (25p) in the 1930s and then to an unprecedented 10 shillings (50p) during the Second World War. It was still over 8 shillings (40p) in the 1960s.

> *I'm spending a year dead for tax reasons.*
>
> **Douglas Adams**

The politics of envy in Britain was running at its highest in the 1960s and 70s. In 1967–8, a special tax of 9 shillings or 45p in the £ was levied so that, allied to the super tax rate of 18s 3d (or 91 per cent), the top rate on 'investment' income was 27s 3d, or 136 per cent tax. During the 1970s, the top rates were 83 per cent on 'earned' income and 98 per cent on what was termed 'unearned' income (i.e. that from investments or rents). Sanity returned in the 1980s, when the standard rate was reduced to 25 per cent and the top rate to 40 per cent in the 1988 Budget.

Ursula Andress

Anyone who has seen it will never forget it – Ursula Andress as Honey emerging from the sea in *Dr No*, the first James Bond film, in a bikini. She was paid less than $10,000 for her role in the film, but the bikini was bought in 2001 for £41,125.

The world's biggest mugging

On 2 May 1990, in Nicholas Lane in the City of London, a courier, John Goddard, was held up at knifepoint and forced to hand over his briefcase. This briefcase held 300 bearer bonds worth no less than £292 million.

The problem for the thief was that all banks were immediately alerted. The certificates therefore couldn't be cashed and became worthless.

—— Tulipomania or, appropriately, —— in Dutch – *Tulpenmoerde*

One of the first nations to develop a modern financial system was Holland, and, perhaps as a result, it was also one of the first to have a boom-and-bust financial drama, when the Dutch enjoyed a few moments of madness with Tulipomania. The tulip was brought from Turkey to Vienna in the mid-16th century. Within a few years it was being grown in Germany, Belgium and Holland, before reaching England in the 1570s. By the early 1600s, tulips were becoming fashionable and when cultivated plants began to produce mutations, excitement about their value began to rise, especially in Holland. The rarest specimens began to sell for thousands of florins, with interest spreading from enthusiasts to permeate the whole of Dutch society.

By 1634, it seemed that almost everyone in Holland was buying or selling tulip bulbs. Furthermore, many were buying not the bulbs themselves but the 'option' to buy or sell. The frenzy mounted. For example, one 'Viceroy' bulb sold for four oxen, eight pigs, twelve sheep, four loads of rye and two of wheat, two hogsheads of wine and four barrels of beer, two barrels of butter and half a ton of cheese plus, finally, a quantity of house furnishings.

A 'Semper Augustus', with vertical red and white stripes over a bluish inner hue, sold for about twice the above, *plus* a carriage and horses. Finally, a single rare bulb was given in France for a successful brewery.

Finally, finally, a shoemaker in The Hague grew a black tulip in the little plot which he, like almost every other Dutchman, had dedicated to tulip-growing. He sold it to some growers from Haarlem, one of whom immediately ground it into dust with his boot. Apparently the growers also had a black tulip, and would have paid anything to protect its uniqueness.

How did such a financial phenomenon happen in Holland in the 1630s?

First, the conditions were right for speculation. The Spanish military threat had finally been removed, the Dutch textile trade was booming, and house prices were rising sharply. Second, the Dutch had a love of flowers, whose beauty provided relief against the flat, dull terrain of their country. The tulip itself was introduced from Turkey (the name comes from the Turkish *tulipan* meaning a turban) by the Imperial Ambassador to Suleiman the Magnificent, Ogier Ghislaine de Busbecq, in the middle of the 16th century. Significantly for the subsequent tulipomania, the plants were initially confined to the gardens of specialist botanists and the nobility, thus giving them an aura of exclusivity.

Furthermore, the varieties were classified by colour and given pretentious, militaristic names – Viceroys, Admirals, Generals. By the early 1600s the more exotic varieties were starting to sell for high prices, and in 1624 a Semper Augustus changed hands for 1,200 florins, a

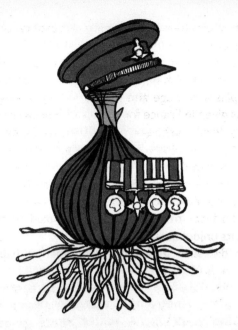

sum which would have bought a small Amsterdam town house. Over the next ten years, trading in tulips progressed to trading in tulip bulbs, which might – or might not – turn into beautiful or, more importantly, unique flowers.

> *Contrariwise, continued Tweedledee, if it was so, it might be; and if it were so it would be; but as it isn't, it ain't. That's logic.*
>
> **Lewis Carroll,**
> ***Through the Looking-Glass***

In 1634 foreigners arrived to join the speculation, and auctions, as well as private transactions, began to flourish.

Then, of course, a market grew up in tulip 'futures', known as the *wind handel* or wind trade. This was the perfect ingredient for an ultimately unstable market. Would the buyer be able to pay the full amount when the time of delivery of the flowers arrived? As the price rose it didn't matter, because they could be sold on by him, or sold to another buyer. But if the prices fell, what then?

In his splendid book, *Devil Take the Hindmost*, Edward Chancellor gives us a measurement of how high the tulips rose: 'The average annual wage in Holland was between 200 and 400 guilders. A small town house cost around 300 guilders and the best flower paintings not more than 1,000 guilders ... According to Gaergoedt's *Dialogues*, a Gouda bulb of four aces rose from 20 to 225 guilders ... a pound of plain yellow Croenen which sold for around 20 guilders rose in a few weeks to over 1,200 (i.e. the price went from the equivalent of one month's pay to five years') ... A contemporary pamphleteer calculated that the 2,500 guilders paid for a single bulb would have bought 27 tons of wheat, 50 tons of rye, four fat oxen, eight fat pigs, twelve fat sheep, two hogshead of wine, four tuns of beer, two tons of butter, three tons of cheese, a bed with linen, a wardrobe of clothes and a silver beaker.'

Almost inevitably, the crash came in February, as spring approached and the buyers were going to have to cough up real money. The actual day was 3 February 1637, when rumours circulated that there were no more buyers. One default was followed by another and then another, and so on. Tulips were suddenly unsaleable.

Those who had loved tulips suddenly hated them. According to Chancellor, the professor of botany at Leyden, Evrard Forstius, was supposed to have been so upset that he couldn't spot a tulip without attacking it with his cane. The tulip became a symbol of luxury, wickedness and seductive illusion, in contrast to the Dutch traits of hard work and dedication.

—— Now you're seriously rich and —— now you're not

Gordon Crawford became the twelfth-richest man in Britain at the height of the dotcom boom in 2000, when his stake in the company he founded in 1986, London Bridge Software (LBS), was valued at £1.3 billion. Not bad for a man who left being a planner for his local council because he thought it was boring. Every bank was using his software to check and assess credit risk and the market gave LBS shares a premium rating.

Then the dotcom bubble burst, and also the banks developed their own software. LBS's shares fell as fast as they had risen, and by 2003 Crawford's fortune had sunk to £58 million. We could all rub along on that, but it isn't £1.3 billion, and by then 617 people in the UK were rubbing along on more.

Of course, most of the world is still either poverty-stricken, poor or struggling to make ends meet, but there are now a lot of wealthy people. By 2001, *The Economist* calculated that there were 7.2 million dollar-millionaires, up from 5.2 million in 1997. By 2006, it must be over 10 million. On top of that, *Forbes* magazine calculated that there were 425 billionaires, 274 in America alone. Again, those numbers will have increased.

Some of these millionaires suffer from 'sudden wealth syndrome', otherwise known as affluenza.

———— Infamous corruption ————

After the Dutch, it was the turn of the British to take leave of their senses with the South Sea Bubble. Set up in 1711 by the government, the South Sea Company did very little for eight years except supply black slaves to Latin America, but then in 1719 it was decided to offer shares to the general public. The PR man who master-minded the promotion was Sir John Blunt, and, just as with the Thatcher government's privatisations, investors (speculators) had to pay only a little at the start and the rest by instalments.

The issue was heavily over-subscribed, and there was an outcry when it was discovered that men of influence had received an extra allocation. In 1719, mesmerised by their success, the government made loans to the public secured on the shares themselves, provided the money was used to buy more stock. If this wasn't the fuel for a short-lived boom and an almighty crash, it's difficult to think of a better one. Pouring oil on the flames was the oleaginous Blunt, who talked of high dividends and the ending of the war with Spain.

Shares in the South Sea Company stood at £128 in early 1720. By March they were £330, by May £550 and by 24 June £1,050. Boom! At that point the government, after all its members had sold at or near the peak, brought in an Act to prevent similar enterprises. Crash! Within weeks the price was back to £175 and by the end of the year it was £124, slightly lower than the starting price. There was, of course, an inquiry. There always is. It dis-covered that some ministers had indeed 'not answered their telephones', and the Chancellor of the Exchequer, the Duke of Argyll, was found guilty of 'infamous corruption' and sent to the Tower. The whole episode triggered a bear market which lasted for a century.

Sir Isaac Newton, among his many other achievements, served as Master of the Mint. In the spring of 1720 he said: 'I can calculate the motions of the heavenly bodies, but not the madness of the people.' He sold his shares in the South Sea Company, having made £7,000 (£770,000 in today's money), a solid profit of 100 per cent. However, the shares took off during the late spring and summer, and he couldn't resist the temptation to buy back in, a decision which cost him £20,000 or £2.2 million in today's money.

In contrast to poor old Newton, who couldn't bear to talk of the South Sea stock ever again, Thomas Guy, a bookseller dealing in bibles and books of common prayer – as well as buying sailor's tickets (credit notes issued by the Navy in lieu of pay) at deep discounts – made a fortune out of South Sea Company shares. In April 1720 his holding was worth £54,000, but over the following two months he sold it for £234,000 – about £25 million in today's money. To the benefit of generations of Londoners since, he founded and endowed Guy's Hospital.

Another successful speculator was Sarah, Duchess of Marlborough, who made a profit of £100,000 (no less than £10 million in today's money). She wrote to a friend: 'Every mortal that has common sense or that knows anything of figures sees that it is not possible by all the arts and tricks upon earth to carry £400,000 of paper credit with £15,000 of specie. This makes me think that this project must burst in a while and fall to nothing.' Her descendant, Winston Churchill, who lost almost all his money in the Wall Street Crash of 1929, commented on her 'almost repellent common sense' in taking profits before the South Sea Bubble burst.

At the time of the South Sea Bubble, a member of the House of Commons suggested that Parliament find the directors of the South Sea Company guilty of treason and give the sentence meted out by the Romans at the height of their empire. This punishment decreed that the perpetrators be sewn into sacks with a monkey and a snake and then drowned. In Theodore Dreiser's novel *The Titan*, this punishment was given to cheating girlfriends.

As the price of shares in the South Sea Company was rising into the stratosphere, other entrepreneurial ventures were being offered to a greedy and gullible public. For example, there were schemes …

'For furnishing funerals to any part of Great Britain'

'For trading in hair'

'For a wheel of perpetual motion'

'For assuring seamen's wages'

'For insuring and increasing children's fortunes'

'For the transmutation of quicksilver into a malleable fine metal'

And Puckles' Machine Company would revolutionise warfare by firing square shot. Most imaginative of all was the gentleman who took an office in Cornhill in the City to promote 'a company for carrying on an undertaking of great advantage, but nobody to know what it is'.

Parliament, waking up to the harmful speculation, banned many bubble companies, such as those …

'For supplying the town of Deal with fresh water'

'For encouraging the breeding of horses in England'

'For making iron and steel in Great Britain'

'For buying and selling estates, and lending money on mortgage'

'For paving the streets of London'
'For the importation of Swedish iron'

All of these sound perfectly reasonable ventures, but such was the belated concern of the authorities that sensible companies were banned along with manifestly speculative or fraudulent ones.

> *A criminal is a person with predatory instincts who has not sufficient capital to form a corporation.*
>
> **Howard Scott**

Once the bubble did burst, there were the usual recriminations. The House of Commons passed a Bill to confiscate the profits that the directors had made during 1720, and over £2 million (more than £200 million in today's terms) was raised, including £96,000 (£9.6 million) from the estate of Edward Gibbon, grandfather of the great historian who wrote *The History of the Decline and Fall of the Roman Empire*.

People have short memories and are usually quickly lured into another get-rich-quick mania. However, the next one to make big waves didn't arrive until the middle of the 19th century, when railways became the quick road to riches – or the workhouse, depending on your timing.

Nor were stolid Victorians averse to a little madness themselves. On 27 September 1825, rail transportation became a reality when one of George Stephenson's locomotives ran from Darlington to Stockton in the north-east of England, carrying 450 people at fifteen miles per hour. The businessmen of Manchester and Liverpool quickly financed a railway line between the two great cities, and Stephenson's *Rocket*, with its speed of 36 mph, won the competition for the locomotives to pull the trains. The building of railway lines spread rapidly throughout Britain and Europe, and by June 1845 plans for over 8,000 miles of new railway were being considered by the Board of Trade. By this time, new schemes for lines were appearing at the rate of over ten a week.

As with tulips and South Sea shares, it seemed that everyone from the richest to the poorest was speculating in railway company shares, and, as usual, many of them were doing it not only with money they could ill afford to lose, but with money they didn't even possess. Emily and Anne Brontë invested in the York and North Midland (sister Charlotte was more circumspect and advised them to sell before the bubble burst). As Edward Chancellor wrote in *Devil Take the Hindmost*: 'By late summer 1845, speculation was reaching a climax. Certain railway scrip showed a 500 per cent profit, and interest on loans against railway stock was being charged at rates of up to 80 per cent. "Direct" routes between towns served only by branch lines became the craze. Foreign railways were projected around the globe, from British Guyana to Bengal. Over a hundred railways were planned for Ireland. A Railway Club was established in the West

End, where "gentlemen of all ranks, connected with railway projects, may daily meet for the interchange of information." In September, over four hundred and fifty new schemes were registered, and a single issue of the *Railway Times* contained over eighty pages of prospectus advertisements. In just ten days in early October, over forty new schemes with a capital requirement of £50 million were announced.'

And then in the autumn, the bubble burst. The companies needing cash for construction asked for the money that was on 'call' from subscribers and, of course, many of them didn't have it. On 14 October (October always seems to be the month for bursting bubbles – think of 1929 and 1987), *The Times* reported that a Mr Elliott had shot himself in Hyde Park and that railway company certificates had been found in his pocket. Two days later, the Bank of England raised interest rates (only to 3 per cent, but markets don't like rising interest rates). Railway shares plummeted in London and then, as – perhaps fittingly – the news travelled by rail to the provinces, they plummeted there too. The *Newcastle Journal* wrote: 'The transition has been from unexampled buoyancy to almost hopeless depression – from an unnatural and unstable elevation to the lowest depths of suspicion and distrust.'

There was a difference between the railway mania of the 1840s and the South Sea Bubble of the 1720s. First, the bursting of the South Sea Bubble appeared to have little impact on the general economy of the country, whereas the collapse of many of the railway companies and the sharp decline of the share prices of those that survived, allied to the continual calling forth of money from those that had committed to shares, contributed to a full-blown financial crisis in 1847.

The historian John Francis wrote: 'No other panic was ever so fatal to the middle class. It reached every hearth, it saddened every heart in the metropolis. Entire families were ruined. There was scarcely an important town in England but what beheld some wretched suicide. Daughters delicately nurtured went out to seek their bread. Sons were recalled from academies. Households were separated: homes were desecrated by the emissaries of the law. There was a disruption of every social tie. The debtors' jails were peopled with promoters; Whitecross Street was filled with speculators; and the Queen's Bench was full to overflowing.'

On Monday, 17 October 1847 (here we go again in October), what was described as a 'week of terror' began in the City. Every type of stock and share fell sharply as people moved into that supposed safe haven, gold. On Tuesday, the Royal Bank of Liverpool failed (and Liverpool then was a far more important city than it is today), followed by three other banks. The Bank of England's reserves dwindled to a point where it was considering closing its doors.

As ever, scapegoats were sought, and in this case it was the Railway King, George Hudson. Hudson had begun his railway involvement in 1827 by investing a £30,000 bequest (£3 million today) in the North Midland Railway Company. By 1844, he controlled 1,000 miles of railway, and in the momentous year of 1845 he was elected Conservative Member of Parliament for Sunderland.

He celebrated by buying a 12,000-acre estate from the Duke of Devonshire for just under £500,000 (£50 million), and he bought one of the largest private houses in London, the five-storey Albert Gate mansion in South Kensington. The shareholders of one of his companies even subscribed to have a statue of him erected.

When the crash came and the search for a scapegoat was in full cry, it was revealed that Hudson had indeed cut some corners in building up his companies. He escaped prosecution but was forced to flee to the Continent to escape his creditors. He died in 1871 leaving just £200 (£20,000).

—————— **The Crash of 1929** ——————

And then, of course, madness and greed flared up again in the 20th century, first with the boom and bust in America in the 1920s.

In 1920s America, many believed – as others before them in different countries and different eras – that a new and sure-to-last prosperity had arrived. Some were reassured by the setting up of the Federal Reserve System in 1913, with its ability to control interest rates and help banks in times of crisis. They assumed it would be able to iron out the booms and slumps which had so bedevilled industry and commerce in the 19th century.

> *I have made millions but they have brought me no happiness.*
>
> **John D. Rockefeller**

The whole atmosphere in the USA in the 1920s was conducive to a boom in the stockmarket. The President who took office in 1924, Calvin Coolidge, was no ideologue. He was lazy, and his only belief appeared to be that businessmen should be left to get on with what they were good at, which was business. As he said: 'The business of America is business.'

His Treasury Secretary, Andrew Mellon of the Mellon banking family, agreed with him. Anti-trust laws were relaxed, allowing more big corporation mergers and takeovers, the top rate of tax was cut from 65 to 32 per cent, corporation taxes were cut to 2.5 per cent and capital gains taxes were slashed. These measures provided a wonderful recipe for a bull market – the rich had more money to invest, corporations reported higher after-tax earnings, and more of the gains from investing in those companies could be retained. To add fuel to the fire, the Federal Reserve lowered interest rates in 1925 and again in 1927.

And there was the new technology, notably motor cars and the radio. During the 1920s, the number of passenger cars on the roads of the USA rose from 7 million to 23 million. The share price of General Motors, the largest car manufacturer, rose tenfold between 1925 and 1928. Sales of radio sets rose from $60 million in 1922 to $843 million in 1928. The stock price of the Radio Corporation of America (RCA), the largest manufacturer of radios *and* the leading broadcaster, rose from $1½ in 1921 to $85½ in 1928 and on to $114 in 1929. Other new technologies to benefit were the aircraft and film industries.

> *If I had my life to live over again, I'd be a $30 a week librarian.*
>
> **Andrew Carnegie**

As the long bull market on Wall Street reached its climax in 1929, everyone was into the never-ending boom in stocks – rich and poor, bankers and bootblacks, dowagers and their cleaning women, teachers and students, nurses and barbers, clergymen and taxi-drivers.

A stock that typified the boom and bust of Wall Street and consequently the USA – and, some would say, consequently the world – was RCA. When it was listed on the New York Stock Exchange on 1 October 1924 it sold at $26\frac{5}{8}$ a share. Radio was obviously a growth area, and the stock became one of the most actively traded. Moreover, it fluctuated wildly. It reached $77\frac{7}{8}$ in early 1925 but by March 1926 had retreated to $32. It then marched to a new high of $101 in 1927 before falling back to $85\frac{1}{4}$ in February 1928. Then it took off and reached $420 by December 1928. It was then split so that shareholders received five shares for every one they held. The price of the new shares reached $114\frac{3}{4}$ in 1929 (equivalent to $573\frac{3}{4}$ in the original shares). By 1932 they were $2\frac{1}{2}$.

—— You don't need to jump – it's —— only money!

The Crash of '29 brought forth stories of spectacular suicides and, of course, there was some slightly forced humour. The comedian Eddie Cantor, who had lost $1 million himself, told his audience the story of two speculators leaping off the 59th Street bridge holding hands because they held a joint account.

When people checked into Manhattan hotels, the

receptionists would ask: 'You wanna sleep in it or jump from it?'

Many of the stories were apocryphal. But Winston Churchill, who also lost a lot of money in the Crash (£10,000 or £550,000 in today's money), and who happened to be in New York at the time, wrote on the day after Black Thursday: 'Under my window a gentleman cast himself down fifteen storeys and was dashed to pieces, causing a wild commotion and the arrival of the fire brigade.'

Some of the accounts of hardship were only too accurate. Here's how Edward Chancellor in *Devil Take the Hindmost* described some of the tragic personal stories: 'As the nation sank into depression, the apotheosis of the businessman came to an end. In March 1932, Ivar Kreuger, the Swedish Match King, committed suicide in a Paris hotel after his business empire collapsed under the weight of debts and the discovery of Kreuger's own frauds. The following month, Samuel Insull's Middle West Utilities went into bankruptcy, and Insull fled the country (he later returned to face trial and was acquitted of fraud). The directors of the Goldman Sachs Trading Corporation were put on trial for wasting the company's assets. Charles Mitchell was forced to resign from the National City Bank, whose share price fell to 4 per cent of its 1929 peak, and in 1934 he was tried for income tax evasion. William Crapo Durant was sold out by his brokers in late 1930 and declared bankrupt in 1936 with debts of nearly a million dollars. He found temporary employment washing dishes in a New Jersey restaurant. Jesse Livermore, who had made his first fortune in Wall Street during the 1907 panic, lost an estimated $32 million before being declared bankrupt in March 1934.

Six years later, Livermore blew his brains out in the washroom of the Sherry-Netherland Hotel in New York. When the market touched bottom in 1932, Radio Corporation of America was selling for $2.50 a share, down from $114 three years earlier. Mike Meehan, the Radio specialist on the New York Stock Exchange, was reported to have lost $40 million in the crash. His seats on the Exchange were put up for sale and his brokerage offices on the transatlantic liners were closed down. In 1936, Meehan entered a lunatic asylum.'

—— Not only stocks but land ——

A warning of the Crash of '29, which wasn't heeded, came earlier in the decade in Florida, where speculators jumped on the property bandwagon. After the end of the First World War, real-estate agents began to push the attractions of Florida, where the temperature in winter was 35 °F warmer than freezing New York. It was a perfect place for a holiday home. As the attractions were appreciated, land values started to rise, and the buyers who actually wanted a house or apartment in Florida were joined by those who merely wanted to make a capital gain, a quick buck.

Trading was easy, dangerously easy, as many didn't even buy the land – only the right to buy the land, and for this they had to put down only 10 per cent of the value. These rights were called 'binders'. Some bought and sold and made a fortune. Others were left with the right to buy such gems as land 'on the shore' – actually fifteen miles inland; 'near Jacksonville' – actually 65 miles inland;

and 'near the fast-growing town of Nettie' – which didn't exist.

The great political evangelist William Jennings Bryan gave lectures on the beauty and healthy climate of Florida. Guess who paid his lecture fees? A real-estate company.

In 1926 the Florida land market crashed, helped by two hurricanes which killed 400 people and left a trail of devastation. It was a warning to the Wall Street speculators, a warning which most chose to ignore.

A.J.P. Taylor, in his book *English History 1914–45*, wrote: 'English people were not too poor to lend abroad; they merely did not want to do so. An Englishman who put his money into tin mines, Argentine rails, or foreign government-bonds in the 1920s found himself in the 1930s with a stack of worthless, highly decorative share certificates. An Englishman who built a fine modern house found himself with a fine modern house.'

In the 1920s, American people bought a lot of decorative paper, encouraged to do so by their own banks. In spite of reports that Peru was careless in fulfilment of moral obligations and had a long history of bond defaults, the National City Bank and J.W. Seligman organised $100 million of Peruvian bonds in 1927 and 1928.

——— Listen to shoeshine boys ———

Some emerged relatively unscathed. For example, Rockefeller saved his fortune in 1929 by selling out just before the Crash. How the hell did he know? Because on the way to his office one morning he stopped to have his shoes cleaned, and the shoeshine boys were discussing stock prices. If shoeshine boys were playing the market and selling, who was left to buy? A shoeshine boy didn't make a lot of dough. In other words there has to be liquidity, and that liquidity was strained to breaking-point. There was nothing left to push the market up. In the 1987 Crash it was Sir James Goldsmith who saw the writing on the wall; he sold £150 million worth of shares just before it happened. Jammy.

And what were the results of the Crash of '29? Some economists have tried to downplay its effects, maintaining that the Great Depression of the early 1930s was inevitable, or was a result of other factors. For example, Milton Friedman, the monetarist economist beloved by Margaret Thatcher, claimed in his *Monetary History of the United States* that: 'The stock market crash in 1929 was a momentous event, but it did not produce the Great Depression and it was not a major factor in the Depression's severity.'

Friedman blamed the US Federal Reserve for its restrictive monetary policy, which meant that the stock of money in the USA declined by a third between August 1929 and March 1933. This lesson has been well learnt, and you will notice that every time there's a sharp fall in stock and share prices – for example in 1987 and 2000 – central banks, especially in the USA and the UK, lower interest rates to increase liquidity.

The truth is: the Crash was not *the* cause of the Depression but it was certainly one of them. This is what a witness to the hearings before the Committee on Labor told the House of Representatives in 1932:

'During the last three months I [Oscar Ameringer of Oklahoma City] have visited as I have said some 20 states of this wonderfully rich and beautiful country. Here are some of the things I heard and saw. A number of Montana citizens told me of thousands of bushels of wheat left in the fields uncut on account of its low price that hardly paid for the harvesting. In Oregon I saw thousands of bushels of apples rotting in the orchards. Only absolutely flawless apples were still saleable, at from 40 to 50 cents a box containing 200 apples. At the same time, there are millions of children who, on account of the poverty of their parents, will not eat one apple this winter.'

'While I was in Oregon the Portland *Oregonian* bemoaned the fact that thousands of ewes were killed by the sheep raisers because they did not bring enough in the market to pay the freight on them. And while Oregon sheep raisers fed mutton to the buzzards, I saw men picking for meat scraps in garbage cans of the cities of New York and Chicago. I talked to one man in a restaurant in Chicago. He told me of his experience in raising sheep. He said that he had killed 3,000 sheep this fall and thrown them down the canyon, because it cost $1.10 to ship a sheep, and then he would get less than a dollar for it. He said he could not afford to feed the sheep, and he would not let them starve, so he just cut their throats and threw them down the canyon.'

'The roads of the West and Southwest teem with hungry hitchhikers. The camp-fires of the homeless are seen along every railroad track. I saw men, women, and children walking over the hard roads. Most ... were tenant farmers who had lost ... all in the late slump of wheat and cotton.'

'The farmers are being pauperized by the poverty of industrial populations and the industrial populations are being pauperized by the poverty of the farmers. Neither has the money to buy the product of the other; hence we have over-production and under-consumption at the same time and in the same country.'

In Europe, many economies were dependent on Ameri-can loans and investment. The Crash meant that many short-term loans were recalled and investment dried up. In Austria in May 1931, the Creditanstalt, the country's largest commercial bank, closed its doors. This caused panic and a run on the reserves of not only Austria but, more significantly, Germany. The general situation in Germany deteriorated rapidly. This is how Edgar Mowrer, the Berlin correspondent of the *Chicago Daily News*, described it:

'These half-orphaned children of disorder, war and inflation, neglected by parents, allowed to grow up unassisted in the world with no sustaining certainty, needed the particular care of society. Instead of which, they, the tender, the unorganised, were the first victims of social readjustment. As they reached the years of activity, they found to their dismay, no places open to them. The young chemist, engineer, teacher, lawyer, doctor, specialist in any branch, even the artisan, found the road blocked by his father and elder brother. In the resulting cut-throat struggle for employment, the inexperienced inevitably lost. And the hatred of the disinherited swelled monstrously – hatred against the father (according to Sigmund Freud the most fundamental of all hatreds), hatred against a social system that had no place for its young – a system that had accepted from the victorious Allies a treaty that (according to the Nationalists) inevitably meant the castration of Germanism. Here was splendid material for political radicalism. Without the Versailles Treaty these young men would unquestionably have turned against the economic beneficiaries of the system and perhaps succeeded in eliminating them.'

'As it was, with sixty per cent of each new university graduating class out of work (March 1932), with over half of all Germans between the ages of sixteen and thirty unemployed, with a dole system that favoured the elder jobless at the expense of the (presumably) protected youth, young Germany was an easy victim for the patriotic demagogue.'

'A new group, the National-Socialists, had the clever idea of uniting the militarism desired by the Reichswehr, the anti-Republican hatred of the reactionaries, the anti-Socialist aims popular among the Capitalists, with a new, generous, vaguely socialist fascism.'

Hitler was on his way.

—— **The casualness of call girls** ——

Perhaps that great author, F. Scott Fitzgerald, should have the last word on the Crash of '29. He claimed that the Jazz Age ended with the Crash: 'The most expensive orgy in history is over because the utter confidence which was its essential prop received an enormous jolt, and it didn't take long for the flimsy structure to settle earthward ... It was borrowed time anyhow – the whole upper tenth of the nation living with the insouciance of grand ducs and the casualness of call girls.'

What is inflation?

Governments constantly worry about inflation. This is hardly surprising, because during the last 100 years there have been several nasty bouts of inflation in all developed countries, and one or two horrendous episodes – Germany 1923, Hungary 1945–6 – and several serious ones.

There have been many definitions, but perhaps the best and simplest is 'a sustained rise in the general level of prices'.

The two most important words in that sentence are 'sustained' and 'general'. For example, at an important sporting event such as a cup final the price of a ticket can go through the roof, which is extremely inflationary for someone determined to go to the game. However, it could hardly be described as sustained or general, and it wouldn't be of concern either to the government, the Bank of England Monetary Committee or, indeed, most people.

> *Lenin is said to have declared that the best way to destroy the capitalist system was to debauch the currency. By a continuing process of inflation, governments can confiscate, secretly and unobserved, an important part of the wealth of their citizens … Lenin was certainly right.*
>
> **John Maynard Keynes**

Inflation has also attracted various adjectives to describe its level:

Creeping – most of the developed world in the 1950s and 60s

Trotting – most of the developed world in the 1970s and 80s

Galloping – Britain in the mid-1970s

Chronic – most of South America since the Second World War

Hyper – Germany in 1923, Hungary in 1945–6, Zimbabwe in 2005–6

What is governments' view of this?

On the one hand, they like inflation because governments are always borrowers of money and it means that, in real terms, they have to pay back less, sometimes much less, than they borrowed.

On the other hand, inflation is destabilising and makes people frightened, especially those, the majority, who aren't in a position to protect themselves quickly from the unpleasant effects of rising prices. It tends to reward the less desirable elements of society at the expense of the rest of us solid citizens.

> *Invest in inflation. It's the only thing going up.*
>
> **Will Rogers**

Let them eat cake

Marie Antoinette apparently said to one of her courtiers when told that the mob at the gates of Versailles had no bread: 'Let them eat cake.'

The German government might have said the same in November 1923. This was how the price of a simple loaf of bread escalated between 1918 and 1923:

1918	0.63 Marks
1922	163.15 Marks
January 1923	250 Marks
July 1923	3,465 Marks
September 1923	1,512,000 Marks
November 1923	201,000,000,000 Marks

In Germany in 1923, for a number of reasons connected with the First World War and the way the victorious Allies decided to treat the defeated enemy, inflation took off to an extent unheard of in the developed world, and at a rate almost impossible to grasp.

This was the cost of basic necessities for four weeks for a family with two children aged six and ten:

4 April 1923	433,509 Marks
25 April	463,366 Marks
6 June	981,233 Marks
14 August	8,370,651 Marks
22 October	504,695,395,848 Marks
29 October	1,563,104,700,000 Marks
2 November	15,554,575,000,000 Marks

In the UK, as the chart below shows, inflation is a 20th-century phenomenon.

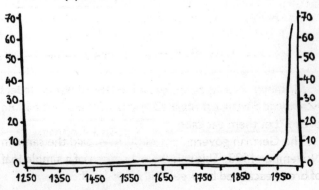

—— Knighthood or jail – depends —— who you work for

In 1919, to help finance the heavy cost of the First World War, the British government floated a huge bond issue, the Five Per Cent War Loan. It was scheduled for repayment 30 years later in 1947, but in 1932, with government revenues low because of the worldwide Depression, interest payments on the War Loan were absorbing no less than 40 per cent of the money raised by income tax.

The government couldn't afford to pay off the loan, so it set out to persuade holders to accept an alternative. Because of the Depression, interest rates had fallen to just 2 per cent; the government offered holders of the 5 per cent loan a conversion to a new security which yielded 3.5 per cent but with no maturity date. The offer was accompanied by a huge publicity campaign urging people to do their patriotic duty in the country's time of trouble. The leading banks were summoned by the Chancellor of the Exchequer and asked to set a good example. All except the Midland agreed, whereupon the Bank of England bought out their share, enabling the government to announce unanimous support.

The result, thanks to inflation, was the eventual reduction of the investment of those who held the loan and who agreed to the conversion, to virtually nothing.

Inflation is one form of taxation that can be imposed without legislation.

Milton Friedman

The government wasn't the only one to cash in on the public's patriotism and gullibility. Horatio Bottomley, a

62

Liberal MP from 1906 to 1912 and an Independent MP when the First World War ended, was also a business entrepreneur. He founded the Victory Bond Club in 1918 and was taking up to £100,000 a day (£5.5 million in today's money). Not only were the funds badly invested, but Bottomley siphoned off large chunks to buy a controlling interest in two newspapers. Bottomley was charged with fraud. Investors in the Victory Bond Club lost all their money, as did those who bought the government's War Loans.

The difference was that most of those in the government who perpetrated the War Loan scandal received knighthoods or were elevated to the House of Lords, whereas Bottomley went to jail.

The incompetence of governments

And, if we need more evidence of the follies of which governments are capable, we need look no further than the notorious Groundnuts Scheme set up just after the Second World War.

Farming is almost always best carried out by farmers acting in an entrepreneurial way. For some reason, governments seem to think that they can run agriculture better, and history is littered with examples of their follies – Europe's Common Agricultural Policy (CAP) being perhaps the prime one. Almost as bad but mercifully less long-lived was the African Groundnuts Scheme, set up in the late 1940s by the idealistic Labour government of Clement Attlee.

In the aftermath of the Second World War, Great

Britain was short of margarine; indeed the whole world was short of edible oils. Britain's colonies in Africa had plenty of available land and plenty of surplus labour. Tanganyika (now Tanzania) was chosen and John Strachey, Minister of Food, set up the Overseas Food Corporation.

Then the problems arose. The necessary bulldozers and tractors were in short supply, so Sherman tanks, of which there were plenty, were converted. But tanks are very heavy and use a great deal of fuel. They are also quite complicated. The African labour couldn't run or repair these tanks. Furthermore, they weren't very keen on being drafted into Strachey's Groundnuts Scheme.

> *Some 25 years ago, you could make a long-distance call on a privately owned telephone system from San Francisco to New York for $28. For that same amount of money, you could send 1,376 letters. Today, you could make the same telephone call for two dollars and a half and for that amount you can only send 41 letters. So the government is investigating the Bell System!*
>
> **Ronald Reagan**
> **when Governor of California**

Various Commissions of Enquiry were put in place, which discovered that the original start-up budget had been greatly exceeded, that there was no longer a shortage of edible oils, and that the annual cost of producing crops worth £100,000 was no less than £600,000. After yet another investigation, the scheme was abandoned in January 1951.

This wasn't Strachey's only disastrous scheme. There was also the Gambian Egg Scheme. And what did the government do? It promoted him to the Ministry of War just as the Korean War broke out.

—— Brussels in generous mood ——

And governments have continued to be silly about farming.

Farmer Oliver Walston told the *Sunday Times* how grateful he was to 'those generous taxpayers who make my life so pleasant': 'I am a happy man. Not just because harvest has been easy this year, not because prices are higher than last year, but because by Christmas I will receive a little brown envelope. The postmark will be Guildford but the cheque inside, for almost £200,000, will come from Brussels. It is my share of the CAP … For every acre of cereals I grow, Brussels pays me £109. For an acre of oilseed rape I am paid £192 and for an acre of peas or beans £157. But there was a price to pay. We have to set aside 15 per cent of our farms and promise to grow nothing on this land. But even here Brussels were in a generous mood. I now receive £138 for every acre I set aside, which amounts to £40,000 on my farm.'

By 2000 there were twelve farmers in Britain receiving cheques from Brussels of over £1 million, and five who received more than £5 million. Farmers didn't have it so easy in Queen Victoria's reign. Here are the prices of wheat per quarter from 1815 to 1910:

	s	d
1815	65	7
1817	96	11
1822	44	7
1831	66	4
1835	39	4
1845	70	8
1850	50	10
1854	72	5
1860	53	3
1870	46	11
1880	44	4
1890	31	11
1900	26	11
1910	31	8

In other words, farmers in 1910 were receiving less than a third of the sum that their great grandfathers received for their wheat nearly 100 years earlier.

> *There are only two kinds of statistics, the kind you look up and the kind you make up.*
>
> **Rex Stout**

Money was vulgar

Land was important.

In 19th-century Britain, land ruled. As Jeremy Paxman put it in his book, *Friends in High Places*:

'Mere money ... was a vulgar, impotent thing. To enter the ruling class you had to have estates. The fifteenth Lord Derby, who owned 69,000 acres of British soil, enumerated the benefits of land-ownership succinctly:

> The objects which men aim at when they become possessed of land may be enumerated as follows: 1) political influence; 2) social importance, founded on territorial possession, the most visible and unmistakable form of wealth; 3) power exercised over tenantry; the pleasure of managing, directing and improving the estate itself; 4) residential enjoyment, including what is called sport; 5) the money return – the rent.

It is a revealing ordering of priorities, and again accentuates the connection between political and social power and the soil.'

'The last comprehensive examination of land-ownership in Britain took place over a century ago. Bateman's New Domesday survey, amplified in 1883 by his Great Landowners of Great Britain and Ireland, proved a spectacular "own goal" for Lord Derby, who had urged Parliament to sponsor and publish the investigation to disprove "wildest and reckless exaggerations" suggesting that most of the country was owned by relatively few people. To his considerable embarrassment, the survey confirmed the exaggerations: three quarters of Britain was owned by seven thousand people. One quarter of England and Wales was in the hands of a mere 710 citizens. The concentration of ownership was most pronounced in Scotland, where no less than half the Highlands belonged to just fifteen owners.'

Diana Memorial Fund – we charge, not donate

What is deemed to be fair in a society and therefore likely to contribute to the stability of that society? In Sweden, progressive taxation means that the highest earners are paid only about five times the lowest. The UK is different. In 1998, the Trades Union Congress (TUC) published a survey of 362 companies which showed that the average pay of the highest-paid directors (excluding fringe benefits and incentive bonuses) had risen from £204,160 in 1994 to £312,910 in 1997. This had taken them up from twelve times the pay of the average employee to sixteen times. For the FTSE-100 companies (the 100 largest companies listed on the London Stock Exchange), the gap was even wider. The highest-paid directors were receiving £970,000, no less than 48 times the average pay of an employee.

> *Only lawyers and mental defectives are automatically exempt from jury duty.*
>
> **George Bernard Shaw**

Solicitors earning lots of money and irritating the rest of the population isn't a new phenomenon. Shakespeare constantly refers to evil or grasping lawyers. And there were plenty of them in the 16th and 17th centuries. The Dissolution of the Monasteries created a property boom with plenty of deals and litigation. There was one lawyer for every 20,000 people in 1560. By 1640 it was one for every 2,500. Now it's an unbelievable one for every 684.

Ambulance-chasing has yielded rich rewards. The National Health Service now sets aside over £1 billion to meet claims.

The first thing we do, let's kill all the lawyers.

William Shakespeare,
Henry VI, Part 2

In a sports claim, Paul Elliott of Chelsea lost his case against Dean Saunders of Liverpool for a tackle which put him out of the game. Needless to say, the lawyers didn't lose and picked up £500,000.

And plenty of lawyers earn serious money from state-funded legal aid. In 1998, twenty barristers received £190,000 to £320,000 in civil legal aid, while another group received £329,000 to £500,000 in criminal legal aid.

So many solicitors are corrupt, and thefts of money belonging to clients so common, that the Law Society has appointed a former fraud squad officer to its staff to monitor the activities of its members.

In the business sector, the practice of charging by the hour has made many commercial lawyers very rich. In 1998, the top 100 law firms in Britain shared total fee income of no less than £4.34 billion. One quarter of this was generated by the top five firms, whose partners averaged an income of £544,000.

Barristers are even worse, charging up to £1,000 an hour *plus* a daily fee, known as a refresher, of £3,750 for every day in court. The system positively encourages rival barristers to prolong cases. Death and divorce provide a rich seam for them to mine, with emotion overriding judgement and common sense. For example, two brothers went all the way to the High Court in a dispute over toy trains left by their father. They eventually agreed to take one each.

It's difficult to comprehend how, but the lawyers working on the Diana Memorial Fund charged £495,000 for three months' work. Furthermore, according to the media they made no contribution to the fund!

There are three reasons why lawyers are replacing rats as laboratory research animals. One is that they are plentiful; another is that lab assistants don't get so attached to them; and the third is that they'll do things that you just can't get rats to do.

—— Bollinger at £1.35 a bottle ——

How have hotel charges fared in the inflationary atmosphere of the 20th century? Pretty well, is the answer.

At the five-star Royal Bath Hotel in Bournemouth, at tea dances in the 1920s where tea was served by uniformed waiters, the cost was 1s 6d (7.5p or £4 in today's money).

Lunch, dinner, bed and breakfast for two in the 1930s cost 22s 6d (£1.12.5p or £62). A bottle of wine was 6s 6d (32.5p or about £18). This was relatively cheap by today's standards, but the one thing that was expensive compared with today was the telephone. One call was charged at 1s 3d (7p or £3.85 in today's money).

The cheapest bottle of champagne on offer was Le Forestier at 17s 6d (87.5p or £48). A 1929 Bollinger cost 27s (£1.35 or £74). A more modest Medoc cost 4s 6d (22.5p or £12), but a Château Lafite-Rothschild 1925 was 12s (60p or £33).

A brandy in the bar was 2s (10p or £5.50) and a gin and tonic 1s 4d (7p or £3.85).

There were extras on the menu such as caviar at 5s (25p or £13.75) or Whitstable oysters at 8s 6d (42.5p or £23).

On Wednesday 6 September 1939, three days after Neville Chamberlain said: 'and consequently this country is now at war with Germany', the Royal Bath gave a supper dance and cabaret which included the world-famous Bebe Daniels and Ben Lyon. The charges were: for the dancing, 6s 6d (32.5p or £18); for dancing and supper, 11s 6d (57.5p or £31.50).

> *All my shows are great. Some of them are bad. But they are all great. The trouble with this business is that the stars keep ninety per cent of my money.*
>
> **Lew Grade**

In the immediate post-war period, demand for leisure far outstripped supply. The Labour organ, the *Daily Mirror*, railed against 'medium-sized' hotels in Bournemouth charging 12 to 14 guineas a week (guineas, equal to one pound one shilling or £1.05, were an invention, not surprisingly, of the legal profession; but clearly the grasping hotels of Bournemouth weren't averse to using them as well). This was clearly much more than before the war, but at £378 to £440 in today's money, it seems reasonable.

Oh, and the *Mirror* man didn't like being charged 1s 10d (9p or £2.70) for his pint of beer. Again, it doesn't seem out of the way in today's terms.

Once the people were in the hotel, how did it exploit them further? On meals they were restricted by the law, introduced as an emergency measure during the war but continued afterwards (as were many other restrictions) by the Labour government, which forbade any hotel or restaurant charging more than 5s (25p or £7.50) for any meal.

The Royal Bath printed at the top of its lunch and dinner menus: 'By order of the Ministry of Food, not more than three courses may be served at a meal including only one dish of Meat, Game, Fish or Egg. Bread counts as one dish.'

The Royal Bath found this fairly easy to circumvent, making a House Charge of 2s 6d and an Entertainment Charge of the same amount, thereby doubling the cost of lunch and dinner.

Meanwhile, over at another five-star establishment, the Grand Hotel at Eastbourne, the 1908 charges were: for a single room, 5s 6d (27.5p or £30); for a full breakfast, 3s (15p or £16.50); the set lunch was 3s (15p or £16.50); a cup of tea was 6d (2.5p or £2.75); and full board was 12s 6d (62.5p or £70).

The manager, Sam Eeley, was paid £750 (£82,500) plus a bonus of £210 (£23,000). In 1945, the new manager, Dick Beattie, was paid £700 – less than Sam Eeley in

1914. Indeed, it was only about a quarter as much when you consider the inflationary effects of the two wars.

By 1954, with maximum charges on hotel meals removed, the Grand charged 9s 0d (45p or £11) for a three-course lunch.

At the end of the 1950s, attendance at a Grand Hotel dance was 5s (25p or £6) from Monday to Friday and 7s 6d (37.5p or £9) on Saturday. If you took dinner as well, the total charge on any night of the week was 21s (£1.05 or £26).

In the 1960s, with a five-star rating, the Grand was charging £5–8 for bed and breakfast (£100–160) and £7–10 for lunch, dinner, bed and breakfast (£140–200).

—— You've never had it so good ——

About 150,000 people, or half of one per cent of taxpayers, earn more than £100,000. About 500,000 workers, out of 25 million, pay no tax. Two thirds earn between £10,000 and £50,000.

Take away business fat cats, City slickers and professionals, and it's bank managers, policemen and reps who top the league.

The 20th century in Britain, with some short periods of exception, was one of rising prosperity for almost all. The national income in 1914 was £2.5 billion. In 1997 it was £800 billion. Even allowing for inflation, that was four times as much.

Real disposable income, i.e. what people have to spend after inflation and taxes, has risen by an average 2 per cent since the war. It sounds little, but it doubles the standard of living every 30 years, and the war ended 60 years ago.

In the 1950s, only one person in three owned a house, one in four a television set, one in twenty a refrigerator, one in six a washing machine, and one in seven a motor car. Central heating was for the rich. Now more than two thirds of houses are owner-occupied, nine out of ten people have central heating, four in five have a video recorder, nine out of ten a washing machine, three out of four a car. Only one in a hundred doesn't have a fridge.

When Harold Macmillan said just before the 1959 election, 'You've never had it so good' (the double entendre was lost on all but a few), the British owned assets calculated at £66 billion. By the end of the century, the Inland Revenue estimated that they owned market-able assets (i.e. those that can be sold or cashed in) of £2,000 billion.

> *I don't like money actually, but it quiets my nerves.*
>
> **Joe Louis**

— Is money making people happy? —

A significant number are not happy, especially civil servants. A Cabinet Office study estimated that those in the public sector spent a third more time on sick leave than those in the private sector, while the Treasury calculated that absenteeism was costing the taxpayer £6 billion a year. The TUC maintains that one in seven white-collar and one in ten blue-collar workers suffer bullying at work. Many workers can't face the day without drink or drugs. The Chief Medical Officer says that 1 in 28 men and 1 in 12 women are taking anti-depressants. Alcohol Concern says that drunk or drugged employees are costing the economy over £3 billion a year.

> *When I was young I used to think that money was the most important thing in my life. Now that I am old, I know that it is.*
>
> **Oscar Wilde**

— Sir Alf – they don't make them — like him any more

In the 1957 football season, Alf (later Sir Alf) Ramsey, manager of Third Division Ipswich Town, secured promotion to the Second Division (no Premier League in those days, so the Second Division was what's now called The Coca-Cola Championship). To help him do it, he was given a budget of £3,000 (£75,000 today) to spend on new players. Ramsey himself had been transferred to Tottenham Hotspur in 1949 as a player for seven times that figure.

> *Every young man should have a hobby. Learning how to handle money is the best one.*
>
> **Jack Hurley**

Ramsey didn't spend a penny of that £3,000 in his first year. In seven years as manager of Ipswich Town, four of them in the Second Division, one in the First, he spent just £30,000 (£750,000) on players. No wonder they made him manager of England for the 1966 World Cup.

The maximum wage

Ever since 1885, the Football Association had dictated a maximum wage to its clubs and players. In 1905 it was set at £4 a week (£440 today). It was raised to £8 in 1922. When Alf Ramsey played in the 1940s and early 50s, the maximum had been £10 (£250 a week). It was more than the industrial or agricultural wage, but it doesn't look too good against Rio Ferdinand's £110,000 a week.

But Alf won the World Cup for England and didn't give V signs to his fans. Ferdinand gives V signs and will never manage England, let alone take them to victory in the World Cup. Of course, Ferdinand might spend his retirement in a villa in Marbella or La Manga or some other centre of high culture; whereas Alf lived his retirement in a small suburban house in Ipswich. Oh, and Alf was made Sir Alf.

> *The love of money is the root of all evil.*
>
> *The Bible*, Timothy 6:10

Back to the maximum wage. In 1958, the Professional Footballers' Association (PFA, the footballers' union) managed to negotiate it up to £20 per week (£500) during the season and £17 (£425) in the summer. Not all players were on the maximum.

It couldn't last, and in 1961 a players' strike threatened under the strong leadership of Jimmy Hill, the president of the PFA. The immediate effect was a sharp rise, or at least so it seemed then, in the wages of the best players. For example, Fulham and England captain Johnny Haynes became the first £100-per-week footballer, amid great publicity. It was, after all, seven-and-a-half times the average annual wage. Rio Ferdinand's weekly wage, if you can call it that, is about 250 times the average working wage.

But Haynes was the exception. Danny Blanchflower, the captain of Tottenham Hotspur who won the double in 1961–2, was paid only £3,000 a year. According to commentator John Motson, when fellow player Jimmy Greaves was signed by the Tottenham manager Bill Nicholson in 1961, Nicholson deliberately negotiated a fee with AC Milan of £99,999. He didn't want Greaves to be saddled with the burden of becoming England's first £100,000 footballer.

And it wasn't just through their wages that football clubs controlled the players. They could also prevent them transferring to other clubs – until the Newcastle and England player George Eastham took Newcastle United to court in 1963 when they tried to stop him going to Arsenal. The effect was explosive. Whereas Blackpool had paid Stoke City £11,590 and a bottle of whisky in 1947 for the great Stanley Matthews, Newcastle had to pay Blackburn £15 million for Alan Shearer in 1997, plus give Shearer a signing-on fee of £500,000 and guarantee him an income of £1.5 million a year for five years.

—— Rugby's gone professional too ——

No other sport could stand aloof from the lure of money. Rugby Union was forced to go professional in the mid-1990s. Because the crowds were so small, almost all the leading clubs started to lose money. But just as with soccer, there were businessmen with big egos willing to spend some of their fortune on building what they hoped would be the champion team. In rugby's case, it was a north-eastern property dealer called Sir John Hall. He appointed the former England fly-half Rob Andrew as manager on a contract said to be worth £750,000 over five years, and instructed him to build a winning team. One of his first signings was the All Black Va'aiga Tuigemala for £500,000, which eclipsed the £440,000 that the Rugby League club Wigan – professional for 100 years – paid for Martin Offiah in 1992.

In rugby's first season as a professional sport, internationals cost £50–100,000, the next tier £40–70,000, and even players who might not be picked cost £20–40,000. Furthermore, there are fifteen men in a rugby team and injuries are very common. And all this when most clubs are watched by fewer than 3,000 spectators.

—— Gentlemen or Players? ——

Roger Bannister was paid nothing for running the first four-minute mile.

Jack Brabham was paid a £10 a year retainer in the 1950s for competing in and winning the drivers' championship in Formula One. In 1961, his best year, Stirling

Moss competed in 55 races and won £32,700 (about £750,000 today).

In 1968, the first open Wimbledon, the total prize money was £26,150. Rod Laver got £2,000 as men's champion and Billie Jean King £750 as ladies' champion. The total prize money in 2005 was £10,085,510; the men's champion received £630,000 and the ladies' champion £600,000.

In the 1930s and 40s, top footballers – including the greatest of them all, Stanley Matthews – travelled to matches by public bus or train, carrying their own boots.

In 1956, the Surrey and England spin bowler Jim Laker performed the greatest Test Match bowling feat ever, taking nineteen Australian wickets in the Old Trafford Test. Driving himself back to Surrey, he stopped to refresh himself in a pub. People were watching repeats of his performance. He joined them, but no one recognised him.

Laker was, of course, a 'player' as opposed to a 'gentleman', and no sport was more class-ridden than cricket. There was even an annual match between Gentlemen and Players, i.e. those who supposedly were amateurs and those who were professionals. I use the word 'supposedly' advisedly, because the amateurs were usually given inducements that were larger than the wages paid to the professionals.

Indeed, the above-mentioned Jim Laker caused a stir by threatening to turn himself into an 'amateur'. You could tell who the Gentlemen were when looking at the scores in the newspaper, because their initials were included. Hence, Surrey would have 'P.B.H. May' but just plain 'Laker'.

A yardstick of riches was £10,000, which was what the

Prime Minister, Harold Macmillan, was paid in 1960. About a dozen top-flight jockeys earned that and, as we have seen, Stirling Moss earned over £30,000. But footballers were still stuck on the maximum of £20 a week during the season and £17 during the summer, or an annual total of well under £1,000. Furthermore, only about 30 per cent of professionals received it. John Charles, the great Welsh player, earned £15 a week, £12 during the summer, while playing for Leeds in 1957. No wonder he was tempted away to play in Italy, joining Juventus for a then record fee of £65,000.

—— An Arnold Palmer Christmas —— tree – perfect

As we know, sport has moved in the last 100 years from being a pastime for gentlemen to a huge multi-billion-dollar business. Sponsorship and real corporate involvement began in earnest after the Second World War, as the industrialised world became prosperous and leisure hours increased.

With more money flowing into sport and consequently to the leading performers, it was inevitable that managers and agents would offer the deal that they, the agents, would concentrate on maximising the income, while the sportsmen should concentrate on what they did best.

The first truly professional agent was an American, Mark McCormack, and he began in the world of golf. When McCormack started working with the great Arnold Palmer in the late 1950s he realised that Palmer, the leading golfer in the USA at the time, could be marketed just like cornflakes or cosmetics. McCormack also realised the value of top-flight golfers to corporate executives, most of whom played golf. Furthermore, the nature of the sport meant that the self-disciplined became the winners. John McEnroe's tantrums worked well in disconcerting his opponent in tennis. They wouldn't have been allowed in golf.

McCormack marketed Palmer so successfully that in 1967 he was able to write: 'There is no precedent for a sports figure becoming the centre of the kind of merchandising empire that now surrounds Arnold Palmer ... It is now possible not only to play your golf with Arnold Palmer clubs, while dressed from cleat to umbrella tip in Palmer clothes (made in the USA, Canada, New Zealand, Australia, Hong Kong, Japan, France or South Africa), but to have the Palmer image at your elbow in countless other ways. You can buy your insurance from a Palmer agency, stay in a Palmer-owned motel, buy a Palmer lot to build your home on, push a Palmer-approved lawn-mower, read a Palmer book, newspaper column or pamphlet, be catered to by a Palmer maid, listen to Palmer's music and send your suit to a Palmer cleaner. You can have his lather, spray-on deodorant, drink his favourite soft drink, fly his preferred airline, buy his approved corporate jet, eat his candy bar, order your stock certificates through him and cut up wood with his power tools.' In that year, Palmer's name was so strong that the huge J.C. Penney stores chain even considered selling an Arnold Palmer Christmas tree.

> **What is a cynic? A man who knows the price of everything, and the value of nothing.**
>
> **Oscar Wilde**

McCormack never missed a trick in getting his clients into this all-powerful position. When in 1969 Tony Jacklin became the first Englishman to win the Open since Max Faulkner in 1951, McCormack had sold the serial rights of *How I Won the British Open* before Jacklin had even begun his final round. When Jacklin won, McCormack turned the label of the champagne away from the TV cameras. If the champagne producer wanted to cash in on Jacklin's success, they would have to pay for it.

> **You can fool all of the people all of the time if the advertising is right and the budget big enough.**
>
> **Joseph E. Levine**

McCormack eventually took over the promotion of the Wimbledon Championships. It wasn't until the 1970s that the committee woke up to the fact that their Championship fortnight was a golden opportunity for companies to promote their products, and that they should therefore pay for the privilege. Until then, they had been paying Slazenger for the tennis balls they had been using. And until then, Robinson's Barley Water and Coca Cola could be seen next to the umpire's chair without either company paying a penny for the advertising.

By the time McCormack got his teeth into it, the Wimbledon name was worth serious money and, as with Palmer, it became possible to sleep in Wimbledon sheets and under Wimbledon blankets, dry oneself on Wimbledon towels, eat off Wimbledon china, wear Wimbledon clothing and send letters on Wimbledon stationery.

As we said earlier, Roger (now Sir Roger) Bannister was paid not a penny for running the first sub-four-minute mile. The next generation didn't run anywhere for nothing.

As Miles Kington wrote in the *Independent*: 'Highly experienced moneyman needed to handle payments to British athletes. Must not be surprised by fact that athletes unlikely to win race are offered more money than the probable winner. Must not be surprised by differences between appearance money, expenses, exhibition money, real money and trust funds. In fact, must not be surprised by anything in amateur sport.'

The Olympic Games have become a big money-spinner, but only in the last twenty years. The Games in Montreal in 1968 cost the Canadians no less than $1 billion, and ten years later when bids were invited for the 1984 Games, there were only two bidders – Teheran and Los Angeles. This contrasts very sharply with the enthusiasm of London, Paris, Madrid and New York to secure the Games for 2012.

In September 2005, the prize for winning the World Match-play Tournament at Wentworth was no less than £1 million. Despite this, and the fact that the tournament was viewed as one of the most prestigious events – almost on a par with the Open, the US Open, the US PGA and the Masters at Augusta – the three leading players on the American circuit, Tiger Woods, Vijay Singh and Phil Mickelson, didn't bother to accept their invitations to play.

It was all a far cry from the mid-1960s, when Geoffrey Nicholson wrote in his book, *The Professionals*:

'Each year the PGA compiles a list of prize winning; it is complete apart from a few open tournaments that didn't make returns. The Association doesn't like individuals mentioned, but if you break down the list for 1963 you get this anonymous result: one man won £7,209 0s 10d, another £3,720 5s 0d; eight players won between £2,000 and £3,000; twelve won £1,000–£2,000; and fifteen won over £500. The man who was best off, and whom I may name, was Harold Henning; he won £10,000 not for winning, but for holing out in one in the Esso Golden Tournament. Alan Gillies did the same in the Hennessy Tournament, but there, unluckily for him, it was worth only £1,000. The list goes to 130 places, including some visiting players; of these, forty-five won less than £100, two men got £9 10s 0d apiece, and another two nothing.'

'On the debit side, all the players had to pay their own expenses and caddie fees, and golfers don't live poorly – though I suppose they could if they were pushed – when they are on the circuit. If they were absent from their clubs for long, they had to provide a replacement to do their teaching. And their prizes would have been taxed, for they count as earned income (if they had won the money gambling, of course, that would have been another matter).'

'Why, then do they do it? First, from the old competitive urge; as in any sport, amateur or professional, they want to prove themselves. Second, because they hope to get among the top thirty who show a profit for the season; they'll give it a go for a summer or two, and if they fail they'll drop out. And third, because to win £500 just once is more exciting and satisfying, even if it's also more expensive, than earning twice that amount by giving lessons.'

Go back another twenty years and the pickings are even smaller. The first prize in the 1946 Open at St Andrews was £150. It was won by the great American golfer Sam Snead, and when he was told that he had won the equivalent of $600 he said: 'A man would have to be 200 years old at that rate to retire from golf.'

Luckily, he didn't have to wait that long. In 2005, the total prize money for the Open to be held at Carnoustie was over £4 million, and the winner received £700,000. Even the person who came in 78th received £8,000.

——— Get rich by gambling? ———

Here's what William Davis said in his *Money in the 1980s: How to Make It; How to Keep It*:

'Playing cards dart from a dealer's hands like startled sparrows. Nearby banks of slot-machines blink through their multi-coloured eyes and cough up buckets of silver.

A cacophony of clicking, clacking and the murmur of a thousand voices: come on seven … double-zero, double-zero, double-zero …'

'Las Vegas has been called many things – Land of the Golden Fleeced, Lost Wages, Adult Disneyland. It is all of these things and more. Las Vegas is hot, dusty, ungodly, plastic, vulgar and greedy – a city of nude shows and drive-in maternity hospitals, of garish neon signs shouting for attention, of hotels and casinos without clocks, of people on holiday, junkets, weekends, over-nights, all of them on some sort of self-prescribed allowance and all battling with their personal devils to break the bank and go to the limit.'

> *A fool and his money are soon parted. What I want to know is how they got together in the first place.*
>
> **Cyril Fletcher**

'It is a fascinating human zoo, a splendid place for people watching – especially, if like me, you find it easy to resist the lure of blackjack and baccarat table, roulette wheels, clacking dice and clumping one-arm bandits. I have never been keen on games of chance. Oh, I don't mind the occasional flutter on a horse, or on results of an election, but I am not a gambling man.'

'Psychiatrists tell us that few people gamble just for the money – the addict is said to thrive on continuous and perilous decision-making, with frequent disasters that are small enough not to shatter him. I just don't need those kind of kicks. I am also a poor loser, and if there is one thing everyone seems to be agreed on it is that most

86

people lose more money in Las Vegas than they win. Fortunes are made occasionally, to be sure, but many more are left behind. "You cannot wind up a winner over any period of time", says one regular. "Not because Vegas is dishonest: gambling is strictly regulated by the state. It's just that the house percentage, or edge (the odds against winning are always slightly tilted against the gambler and in favour of the casino), cannot be beaten by an honest player."'

'The house percentage ranges from 2 to 14 per cent in every kind of game, and in some, such as Keno, it can go as high as 30 per cent. But it isn't the casinos' only asset. "We live on stupid players", Hank Kovell, an executive of one of the top hotels along the Strip, tells me. It is "stupid players" who make Las Vegas into a twenty-four-hour town – who pay for the lavish entertainment, the ubiquitous strip lighting, the cheap food and drink, and all the other Vegas razzmatazz. It is stupid players who have turned this one-time railway watering stop into an Eldorado for casino owners. Las Vegas has nine million visitors a year and earns more than any other resort community in the world. It does so well that Nevada's 600,000 residents pay no income, sales or inheritance taxes. Who says oil is the only money-spinner?'

'Stupid players don't know when to stop. They cannot, or will not, walk away until they have been badly mauled – and often not even then. Some people claim that gamblers want to punish themselves, but casino men like Kovell (all shrewd observers of human nature) have a simpler and more plausible answer: most amateurs are absurdly over-optimistic. They believe in miracles because they want to believe in miracles. "The gambling spirit", says sociologist Frederick Preston of the

University of Nevada, "is part of the American spirit. It is a sort of plunging ahead and conquering, a kind of boldness, aggressiveness.'"

'If one of the bold spirits loses, he usually has only one thought – get the money back! And because he is pressing like mad, the chances are that he will lose still more. He cannot discipline himself. Some inevitably, also try to cheat. "People resort to the corniest tricks", Kovell tells me. "We've had customers hiding extra cards up their sleeves, would you believe that?" The chances of getting away with it are slight, not only because every table is closely watched by expert supervisors but also because casinos conceal other watchers in the so-called Eye in the Sky, a two-way mirror running the full length of the ceiling. "Cheats", says Kovell, "are quietly escorted to the door."'

'Every casino, of course, is designed to encourage that lucrative stupidity. You can't get to your room – or to one of the hotel restaurants – without passing slot-machines or blackjack tables. And gamblers are shielded from daylight and the running of time so as not to distract them from the primary purpose. Everything, but every-thing, has one aim: to shut out the real world, to sponsor foolish dreams, to offer a way to escape the tedium of slow but secure lives. And you don't have to feel guilty because in Las Vegas everyone else is doing the same thing – or at least appears to be. (And if that isn't enough justification, you can always tell yourself that the sailing of the *Mayflower* to colonise the New World was financed by a lottery in England and that George Washington was an inveterate gambler.) It is a form of infantilism, a return to childhood. And it seems to work particularly well in times of economic recession. As Kovell put it: "When times are bad people tend to say: to hell with it, let's go to Las Vegas."'

'Human nature being what it is, few gamblers ever talk about their losses. No one wants to look stupid. And the casinos (who naturally welcome this reluctance to concede defeat) try to ensure that there are no tell-tale pictures: photography is strictly forbidden. "We get all sorts of people here", says Kovell. "Stockbrokers, investment managers, heads of large corporations. Imagine what it would do to their professional reputations if they were seen to be losers."'

> *Part of the $10 million I spent on gambling, part on booze and part on women. The rest I spent foolishly.*
>
> **Hollwood star George Raft,**
> **to his bank manager**

——— It's shares for you – in the ——— long term

With the possibility of sudden downward lurches, should people be investing in stocks and shares? The answer isn't a simple yes or no, because it depends on a number of factors – the amount of money you invest, whether you can afford to lose it, the time-frame, the knowledge you have. Insider dealing (see below) is now illegal but, of course, everyone who invests in particular stocks thinks he has some inside knowledge. Otherwise why would he pick that particular stock? Buying Marks and Spencer because you know retail sales in general are strong is fine. Some thought that Jeffrey Archer buying Anglia TV shares because his wife, Mary, who happened to be a director, had told him that they had received a bid, was not …

> **There are more fools among buyers than sellers.**
>
> **French proverb**

With regard to the amount of money, there are certain fixed costs such as stamp duty and stockbroker's commission, and if you invest small amounts – say £500 here, £500 there – these costs can be a significant percentage and therefore make it harder to turn a profit. There is also what's called the 'spread'. When you see a share in the paper at, say, 450, that's the 'middle price'. If you want to buy, it will probably cost 452, and if you want to sell, 448. So when the price quoted moves from 450 to 460 you won't make 10p per share, because you will have bought at 452 (plus costs) and sold at 458 (plus costs). You probably don't start making money until the 'middle' price appreciates by about 5 per cent.

Can you afford to lose the money? Shares are a reflection of a business. As we all know, businesses can do well and the shares should therefore go up. They can do badly and the shares will probably go down. They can go bust and you will lose *all* your investment.

The time-frame. Unless you have plenty of money and can afford to lose some of it, the time-frame is probably the most important factor in deciding whether to invest in shares. If you look at the charts below, you'll see that they show the Dow Jones Index of 50 leading shares in the USA from 1929 to 2005. You'll see that the Index plunged from its heady 381.71 in early September 1929 to a mere 41 in early 1933. At that point, it looked as though the world was about to end, and indeed for many it was, because Adolf Hitler had just become Chancellor in Germany.

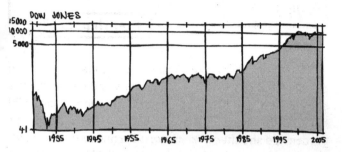

However, taking Rothschild's view that you *buy* when there's blood in the streets, it was a great buying opportunity, taking both the short-term and the long-term views. The index leapt up in the next few months and carried on going up sharply for the next five years; and in the long-term view, it progressed from 41 to 11,700 – a rise of 285 times – by spring 2000.

> *There are only two emotions in Wall Street: fear and greed.*
>
> **William Le Fevre**

If you were eighteen years old in March 1933 and had put $10,000 in Dow stocks, you would have been able to sell them when you were 85 in the year 2000 for $2,850,000. Even allowing for inflation, that's a very substantial gain.

Most of us can't think in such long time-frames, so let's look at some shorter periods. First, if you had been, say, 25 in 1929 and had invested your $10,000 at the top of the market, you would have had to wait until 1954 – when you would have been 50 – to get your $10,000 back, and of course $10,000 wouldn't have bought in 1954 what it bought in 1929. You can see that world wars aren't good for business either, though, as it happens, the best bull market on the London Stock Exchange in the whole of the 20th century took place during the Second World War. The Financial Times 30 (the equivalent of the Dow 50) had plunged from 100 in 1935 to 41 on the eve of the El Alamein battle in 1942. It was, as Rothschild would have known, a great buying opportunity, except that this time it was blood in the sand rather than in the streets.

The Index rose more than threefold to reach 146 in 1945. However, it then moved sideways for the rest of the 1940s as Britain came to terms with the cost of winning the war. It revived again in the 1950s after business was set free by Churchill's 'bonfire of controls', doubling in the second half of the decade from 180 in 1956 to 360 in 1960. But the financial difficulties of the Labour administration in the mid-1960s saw a plunge back to 285 in November 1966.

The Conservative government of Edward Heath came to power in June 1970 and was determined to get the economy growing, whatever the consequences for the balance of payments and inflation. Easy credit was made available, business boomed, and from February 1971 until June 1972 there was a bull market in which the Index rose from 300 to 540. Thereafter the problems came thick and fast. Interest rates were raised to try to stem the rise of inflation, and then OPEC flexed its muscles, cutting back on the supply of oil and raising its price five-fold. There were many damaging strikes, most notably by the miners, and the economy contracted sharply. Investors took fright and the Index retreated week-by-week from November 1973 until January 1975, reaching a low of 146 on 6 January. This was pretty well where it had been in 1945, 30 years earlier. In real terms it was much lower.

As I said earlier, timing is important. You wouldn't have been impressed if you had bought the Index when you were demobbed in 1945 and wanted to cash in your investment as you contemplated retirement in 1975. To add to your woes, the post-war years were quite infla-tionary, so a £ in 1945 was worth about 50p by 1975. Furthermore, 1975 itself was the worst year for inflation in Britain's history, with prices rising by over 25 per cent.

Provided your nerve remains strong, the way to suc-ceed in the stockmarket is to expect to lose in bad years but to keep investing, because your gains in good years should outweigh your losses, provided, as we have seen, that you have a long time-frame. For example, there was a serious downward lurch in all the stockmarkets of the world in October 1987 which effectively, in the short term, erased many of the gains of the Reagan/Thatcher bull market of the previous five years. If, at that time, you had decided you had had enough of the rollercoaster of investment in shares and had put your money in the bank, that would have been one of the worst investments of your life. From October 1987 to March 2000 the Dow Jones Index rose from 1700 to 11700, and after retreat-ing in the early years of the 21st century is approaching 11000 again.

In London, the Financial Times 100 Share Index (the 'Footsie', which has taken over from the FT 30 as a measurement of the stockmarket, generally being a more broadly-based index) rose from 1500 to 6900 and is still around 5700.

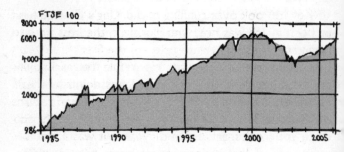

John Maynard Keynes, the greatest and most influential economist of all time, was also a shrewd and gutsy investor. This is what another economist, Roger Bootle, wrote about him in his *Money for Nothing*: 'Keynes – man of affairs extraordinaire, civil servant, patron of the arts, and the greatest economist of the twentieth century – was very nearly wiped out twice in his investing career. At the end of 1927 Keynes's assets totalled £44,000, the equivalent of £1.2 million (roughly $1.8 million) in 2003 prices. But in 1928 he was long on several commodities – rubber, corn, cotton, and tin – when the markets turned sharply downwards. To cover his losses he was forced to sell shares in a falling market. By the end of 1929 his net worth was down to just under £8,000, £220,000 ($330,000) in 2003 prices.'

'Despite these losses, Keynes died a rich man. Overall, he was a sophisticated and successful investor and speculator, on his own and King's College Cambridge's account. He is said once to have been spied measuring up the nave at King's College Chapel to see if it would be big enough to accommodate a large amount of grain, of which he might have to accept delivery if his bull position in the futures market could not be closed out before expiry.'

'Keynes took over running of the King's College fund in 1928, which was not, with hindsight, the best time to begin any investment enterprise. In the first three years he did far worse than the market. While the market was down 36 per cent, the King's fund was down by a half. However, in the next five years Keynes achieved returns of between 33 and 56 per cent per annum, easily out-doing the stock market. On the whole it was a fantastic performance. Interestingly, had Keynes been a profes-sional fund manager operating under today's conditions he would surely have been sacked after a year or two; in fact, probably just as the market was about to turn.'

— I've sold everything except Intel —

Every so often (with some people, once a day), the lust for easy riches grabs hold and rational thinking is abandoned.

In the 17th century it was Holland where tulips took on a golden glow, in England in the early 18th century it was islands in the South Seas, and in the 19th century, again in England, it was railways. In the USA in the 1920s it was the new technologies of roads and communications, and recently in all developed countries it was the information superhighway. This latest bubble was called the dotcom boom.

> *There is nothing like the ticker tape except a woman. Nothing that promises hour after hour, day after day, such sudden developments; nothing that disappoints so often or occasionally fulfils with such unbelievable, passionate magnificence.*
>
> **Walter Gutman**

Nowhere was it more exciting than in the US. In early 1994, the Dow Jones index stood at 3400. The Dow Jones is a measurement of the average price of 50 leading shares on the New York Stock Exchange; so, as the prices of those alters, so does the Index. It had already come a long way from the 800s of 1982. Indeed, I remember talking to the owner of an electrical store on Third Avenue in Manhattan in May 1994 while my son bought a camera, and him saying to me: 'Stocks are too high. I've sold everything except my Intel.'

He was right to hold on to Intel, but wrong about the rest of the market. By the start of 2000, the Dow had risen from the 3400 of 1994 to 11700. Even more striking was the NASDAQ index, which reflected the high-tech stocks more accurately. In 1994 it was less than 500. In March 2000 it broke through 5000.

> *How did I make my fortune? By always selling too soon. Sell, regret – and grow rich.*
>
> **Nathan Rothschild**

Then came the inevitable crash. The Dow suffered quite badly, dropping from that 11700 to 7300 in 2002, but the NASDAQ went into free-fall, dropping from over 5000 to 1000 in early 2002. It has since recovered to 2000, but my stockbroker, who is about 40, doesn't think it will reach 5000 again in his working lifetime. He may be right, but we shouldn't underestimate the irrational exuberance and greed of investors, whose memories of the bloodbath of 2000–02 will fade.

Some of the individual stock falls were amazing. A US company called Chemdex, later renamed Ventro, saw its share price fall from $239 in February 2000 to 37 cents in April 2001.

——————— Toys in the fast lane ———————

If you invest in the stockmarket you must also remember that there's a world of difference between what a company is *actually* worth and what the market perceives it to be worth – or what people are prepared to pay to have a stake in it. In the late 1960s British Motor Holdings, the amalgamation of most of the famous British car-makers from Austin to Morris to Triumph to Jaguar, was producing more than a million real motor cars a year from factories all over the country, and employing 200,000 people. In spite of all these assets, BMH was valued on the stockmarket at less than Lesney, the company that made Matchbox toy cars.

The market saw BMH as an over-manned, badly managed, heavily unionised dinosaur producing poorly designed cars at a loss. It perceived Lesney as a well-managed, lean manufacturer producing well-designed products at a very great profit. The market was right about BMH – it went bust in the mid-1970s, was rescued by the taxpayer and eventually called the Rover Group, was sold to British Aerospace, then to BMW, then to a private group of investors for £1, and finally to the Chinese. But in the long run the market was wrong about Lesney, because in the early 1980s it too went bust and was picked up by a Hong Kong company. But there's no long run in the stockmarket. The people who had pushed Lesney's shares to massive heights and a ridiculous price earnings ratio (a measurement of a company's profits) had long gone. As the mercurial one-time stockmarket guru Jim Slater said: 'A good long-term investment is a short-term investment that has gone wrong.'

Despair of the soup kitchen

Most people don't invest in stocks and shares, so what does it matter if the stockmarkets of the world rise euphorically or crash sickeningly?

As Roger Bootle points out in his book *Money for Nothing*: 'In the 1920s, the American stock market surged on a mood of boundless optimism about the technological advances of the time. However, it all went much too far and in 1929 came the Great Crash. Shortly afterwards, America was plunged into the Great Depression. Optimism about new technology gave way to the despair of the soup kitchen and dole queue. In the 1980s, Japan was a miracle economy and its stock market soared – before collapsing into a decade-long slump, taking the economy with it. The stock market's importance at these critical times should not be surprising, for it is capitalism's hinge, linking present and future.'

'Now we all have to live with the consequences of recent stock-market excesses. The bursting of the bubble has left wreckage strewn across the economic system. And the wreckage in the financial system is deeply shocking. Over the period 2000–2002, the value of all the shares in the world fell by a total of $13 trillion – $13 million million or $2,000 for every man, woman and child on the planet. From pensions to insurance policies to ordinary savings, the implications are only now beginning to hit home. In the UK, the value of the so-called with-profits-funds held by life assurance companies to cover long-term savings and personal pensions fell by about £50 billion (about $75 billion) in 2002 alone – equivalent to £1,000 ($1,500) for everyone in the country.'

——— **Peter – the private punter** ———

In his early forties, happily married with three sons, Peter is a public school and minor Oxbridge college product. As you might imagine, he plays golf. He's not directly involved in the City, but he is fascinated by it. He pores over the *Financial Times* and the City pages of the serious nationals. Managing Director of his own company, he can usually lay his hands on the equivalent of about £200,000 for speculation, and over the years he has made some awful boobs, though he has had the odd success.

He believes that his major handicap is lack of inside information and lack of bottle. Peter was a devout Thatcherite. His heart and mind are in the right place, but he's no match for the Darrens who bask lazily in the warm waters lapping the City shores.

Nevertheless, he has learnt enough about the market over the years to know that you can make money in bear markets just as you can in bull markets. He has never done so himself because, like a rabbit in a car's headlights, he becomes paralysed when prices fall and holds on to shares because he thinks the market is treating them unfairly. As he bought them at 168, they must be wildly undervalued at 107.

He once tried to sell short – he was in the West Car Park at Twickenham when one of his friends from the Midlands told him that Crompton Parkinson, the light-bulb manufacturers, were going bust. The price was 25p and Peter saw the chance to make a quick killing. First thing on Monday he rang Charles, his broker, and asked him to sell 10,000 on his behalf.

'Fine', said Charles, who knew that Peter didn't have any Crompton Parkinson shares. It's not strictly illegal to sell shares you don't own, but it's frowned upon; and it's risky, because you will have to buy the shares at some point and the price may rise. Peter was delighted to get the 25p price – he thought he might get only 23p. All he had to do now was wait for Crompton Parkinson to turn the lights out as they left the building, and he could buy the shares at a nominal 2p, giving himself a nice little earner of around £2,300. Not bad for a Saturday afternoon, even if England had lost again. On Tuesday he was flabbergasted when he read in his *Standard* that Thorn had made a bid, and the price was 125p. There was no way out. He had to buy 10,000 at 125p to cover his sale. He had sold at 25p and now he had to buy at 125p. His bright idea at Twickenham had cost him over £10,000 in 24 hours. As we said before, selling shares you don't have may not be illegal, but it's risky.

Thin markets

When you read in the *Financial Times* market report that Dares Estates rose sharply in a thin market, or more ominously that Acorn fell sharply in a thin market, what does 'thin' mean? Many private investors found out the hard way in October 1987, and again when the dotcom bubble burst in 2000. They had bought all the hyped shares of the previous few months. Peter, for example, had found no trouble buying, though in retrospect it was irritating having to pay 18p for 50,000 Rotaprint when the price in the paper had shown 15p. But what was 3p when the price would be a pound by Christmas? 19 October. Crash. Whoops. Maybe Peter should sell those Rotaprint. They were, after all, a bit speculative. He rang Charles, his broker, and asked him to sell them. The price in the *FT* was 15p, but he was prepared to lose £1,500: after all, he had made several thousands during the year. He was, however, slightly stunned when Charles phoned half an hour later – he had some trouble in getting through to his dealer – and told him that he could sell 1,000 at 12p or 2,000 at 10p. There was no chance of selling 50,000. Peter learnt quickly what he now vaguely remembered reading – for a seller there has to be a buyer. Just because it says in the FT that the price is 15p, that doesn't mean you'll get it for 50,000 shares.

As least he now knows what a 'thin' market is. 'Oh, well', he said, 'I'll hang on. They'll come back.'

Blooper. That was his second mistake. Rotaprint called in the Receiver in February 1988, and the shares which only last September were definitely going to £1 went to nothing. One consolation: Peter can carry forward his £9,500 loss to offset against the capital gains he was sure he was going to make in the future.

Penny shares

Bearing in mind what can happen to marketability in small stocks, known now as gamma and delta stocks, is it worth investing in penny shares? The temptation is strong. Over the years, Peter has been tempted into them for two reasons. First, you get lots for your money. He got 50,000 Rotaprint shares for just over £9,000. If he had put £9,000 into Shell instead, he would have got only 600 shares. Secondly, no one told him – and if they had, he wouldn't have believed them – that Shell was going to £100, whereas he was told by several people that Rotaprint was going to 100p.

Emotionally, to satisfy Peter's greed, it had to be Rotaprint. Logically it should have been Shell. Shell will reach £100 before Rotaprint reaches 100p. After all, now that Rotaprint is in the cemetery, Shell has forever to do it.

But one day Peter will make money on a penny stock. He could have been, but wasn't, in former rag trade company Polly Peck. If he had bought 50,000 in 1980, they would have cost him £2,000. If he had held them for a few months, when the price went from 4p not just to £1 but to £3, his holding would have been worth £150,000. If he had resisted the temptation to sell and held on for two years, when the price rose to £35, his original £2,000 would have become a staggering £1.75 million. Peter was mildly irritated, as we all are, by missing such an opportunity, but he felt better when he was chatting in the bar to a friend. The friend told him that he had bought 25,000 Polly Peck at 6½p. Peter was just going green when he finished the sentence – 'and I sold them next day at 7¼p'. No one ever went broke taking a profit, as they say, but you can miss out on £875,000.

In the event, Polly Peck, having been one of the big successes of the 1970s and 80s, became the subject of one of the major financial scandals of the 1990s. Its boss Asil Nadir, who, with a fortune of £213 million, featured in William Davis's book *The Super Rich* in 1991, fled to Northern Cyprus in a privately chartered aeroplane.

──────── **Dead cat bounce** ────────

If you drop a cat from the top of the NatWest Tower, it will bounce first before falling back to the ground – dead. Similarly, if market prices drop sharply from a great height, they bounce up before dropping again, largely because people who sold short have to buy back to complete the transaction.

This was never better demonstrated than in the Great Crash of 1929 and the subsequent bear market lasting until 1933.

Down sharply went the stocks in October 1929, falling 34 per cent in a month, but then in the spring of 1930 there was a sharp recovery of 24 per cent, accompanied by a large sigh of relief and significant buying again – the cat had bounced – only to be followed by a further plunge in the summer of 1930 and a downward spiral until 1933. By this time, even the bluest of blue chips were a fraction of their price in the summer of 1929 and the market as a whole was down by no less than 85 per cent. The giant ATT fell from $310 to $70, Chrysler from $135 to $5, the mighty Du Pont from $231 to $22, General Electric (a founder of the Dow Jones index and the only survivor to the present day) from $403 to $34, General Motors from $91.75 to $7.75.

Between 1929 and 1933, the gross national product of the USA fell by a staggering 60 per cent, unemployment rose to 12.5 million and over a third of the non-agricultural workforce was looking for a job.

In 1929, just before Armageddon, Herbert Hoover in his presidential nomination speech had declared that the end of poverty was in sight. Marie Antoinette was more accurate when she opined that we would always have the poor. The renowned Yale economist Irving Fisher had announced in the autumn of 1929: 'Stock prices have reached what looks like a permanently high plateau.'

So much for the views of eminent economists!

The crash of '87 – Black Monday

By October 1987, the City was wallowing in an orgy of self-love. The Tories had been voted in for another five years, money – serious money – was there for the taking, the markets were all going up after the usual summer hiccup – then BANG. It all stopped. First New York, then Tokyo and Hong Kong, then London, then New York again, then Hong Kong, Tokyo and Sydney, then London, Paris and Frankfurt all turned into screaming pits of hysteria as the markets lost a year's gains in 24 hours. To exacerbate the situation, the hurricane in Britain three days before prevented many dealers from reaching their screens.

In Britain, shares fell 12 per cent, in Japan 15 per cent, in Australia nearly 25 per cent. In the US, the Dow Jones Industrial Average fell 22.6 per cent, which was nearly twice the fall of 26 October 1929, the first day of the century's most famous crash. More than $500 billion – roughly the same as the gross national product of France – was wiped off the value of US share prices.

It was only twelve years (or 3,000 trading days) since the FT 30 Index had stood at 147. Now it lost 183.7 in a single day. If we thought that was difficult to cope with, the Dow Jones fell by over 500 points, and it was only five years (1,250 trading days) since it had been around 600. But that of course was part of the reason. The indexes had risen a long way, and once punters wanted to cash in some of their profits there could only be one result. Black Monday, 19 October 1987, was so called after Black Monday on Wall Street in October 1929 – which had itself been named after Black Friday, 24 September 1869, when a group of punters tried to corner the gold market, causing a panic which led to a crash and depression.

—— The closest to meltdown I'd —— ever want to get

So many records were broken on 1987's Black Monday – biggest one-day fall, biggest volume, more deals on the New York Stock Exchange that day than in the whole of 1950, etc. – that everyone ran out of superlatives, except that no one thought it was particularly superlative.

Being in the nuclear age, John Phelan, chairman of the New York Stock Exchange, described it as 'the closest to meltdown I'd ever want to get'. Believe it or not, when almost every share collapsed by 25 per cent, several by 50 per cent and the really wild stocks by even 70 per cent, there were one or two which actually went up. One punter had bought some Scottish Ice Rink shares and was offered £2.50 for them on Black Monday, which he turned down. The next day he was offered £5, which he also turned down. He had a smell for it – why would someone offer him £5 for a share when everything else was crashing around his ears? Finally he was offered £20, which he accepted.

—— Blue-Chip Blues and Yuppies ——

The gentleman (American) who invented the ZIP code died a couple of years ago and, reading his obituary, I realised what an influence on the social and economic development of the developed world he had been. The marketeers and, more ominously, the insurance companies, now classify every person according to their ZIP or postcode.

Furthermore, within those codes there are more categories used by those who categorise their targets even more accurately. Hence in the USA there are: Blue Blood Estates, Money and Brains, Furs and Station Wagons. In the middle are Pools and Patios, Two More Rungs, Black Enterprise, New Beginnings, New Melting Pot, Towns and Gowns, Rank and File, Old Yankee Rowers, Bohemian Mix, Gray Power, Young Influentials,

Young Suburbia and Blue-Chip Blues. Further down are Shotguns and Pick-Ups, Levittown and Public Assistance. Don't let's spend much time there, and certainly not on the lowest category, Old-Old.

While on the subject of class and money, here are the nicknames for some other categories:

BOBO	Burnt Out But Opulent
BUPPIE	Black Upwardly-Mobile Professional
DINKIE	Double Income, No Kids
DINKY	Double Income, No Kids (Yet)
DUMP	Destitute Unemployed Mature Professional
GOLDIE	Golden Oldie, Lives Dangerously
GUPPIE	Green Upwardly-Mobile Professional
LOMBARD	Lots of Money but a Right Dickhead
NIMBY	Not in My Back Yard
OINK	One Income, No Kids
PIPPIE	Person Inheriting Parent's Property
PUPPIE	Poncey Upwardly-Mobile Professional
SCUM	Self-Centred Urban Male
SILKY	Single Income, Loads of Kids
SINBAD	Single Income, No Boyfriend, Absolutely Desperate
SINK	Single, Independent, No Kids
SITCOM	Single Income, Two Children, Outrageous Mortgage
WOOPIE	Well-Off Older Person
YAPPIE	Young Affluent Parent
YUPPIE	Young Upwardly-Mobile Professional Person

The dotcom bubble

As with railways in the 1840s and automobiles in the 1920s, the internet in the 1990s was going to transform people's lives (and of course they all did, but not quite as fast, or as profitably for most speculators, as some would have the gullible believe at the time).

> *My problem is reconciling my gross habits with my net income.*
>
> **Errol Flynn**

In 1995 Nicholas Negroponte, author of *Being Digital*, wrote that 'digital living' would reduce everyone's dependence on time and place, close the generation gap and contribute to 'world unification'. Microsoft chief Bill Gates, who *did* make money faster than any speculator could have predicted, wrote in his book, *The Road Ahead*: 'The information superhighway will change our culture as dramatically as Gutenberg's press did in the Middle Ages.'

The impact of internet-based shares on the stock-market was startling. Yahoo!, after only one year of operation and with annual sales of less than $5 million, went to a price on the first day of dealings on the market which made the company worth $850 million.

> *The cares of gain are threefold: the struggle of getting; the frenzy of increasing; the horror of losing.*
>
> **Anonymous**

Edward Chancellor wrote of the dotcom bubble: 'The boom in Internet stocks strengthened in 1998. By the end of the year, the market values of leading Internet companies competed with those of America's largest corporations; the market capitalisation of Charles Schwab, the discount broker with on-line trading facilities, overtook that of Merrill Lynch; eBay, a recently founded on-line auction house, outstripped Sotheby's; and AOL, the Internet service provider, became more valuable than the Disney Corporation. The market capitalisation of Yahoo! was over 800 times its earnings and over 180 times its sales revenue, or $35 million per employee. The share price of Amazon.com, an on-line bookstore, multiplied 18 times during 1998 (despite the company's escalating losses). One fund manager described it as "the most outrageously priced equity in the world," but advised buying the stock nevertheless. The market's response to initial public offerings was particularly feverish. When theglobe.com, an Internet chat service, was floated in mid-November, its shares rose a record-breaking 866 per cent on the first day of trading. On 15 January 1999, Marketwatch.com was floated. Offered to investors at $17, the shares closed at $97.50. Internet stocks were boosted by a shortage of shares available for trading, stock splits, and euphoria surrounding the potential for "e-commerce."'

'Fred Hickey, the editor of *High-Tech Strategist*, called this upsurge "the greatest investment mania since Tulip Bulbs." In late January 1999, Alan Greenspan, Chairman of the Federal Reserve, observed that Internet valuations were "pie in the sky" and that investors were indulging in a lottery, since most Internet companies were doomed to failure and their shares would become worthless.'

On 16 March 2000, as the dotcom boom neared its peak, the Dow Jones index enjoyed its biggest one-day points rise, no less than 499.19 points to 10630.6.

Just over a year later it suffered its biggest one-day fall, 684.81 points, when the market re-opened on 17 September 2001 after the attack on the World Trade Center six days earlier.

———— Bear Hug or Poison Pill? ————

If you're going to punt on the market, you would be well advised to understand some of the buzz-words.

ARBITRAGEUR: A market trader who buys shares in companies which are in takeover situations, usually after a takeover bid is announced, where he believes there will be a higher bid. As Ivan Boesky, the leading arbitrageur during the recent bid cycle, describes it, the arbitrageur 'takes on risks that the rest of the market will not accept'. Arbitrageurs have helped fuel the boom by providing liquidity to the market. Although arbitrage in its classic sense – equating the price of a commodity, currency or stock in one market with that in another – is an old and respected practice, it is relatively new in the corporate world, and still largely confined to Wall Street.

BEAR HUG: A variety of takeover strategy that seeks to hurry target company managements to recommend acceptance of a tender offer in a short period of time. The tactic involves sending target management a letter (later made public) offering to buy shares at a substantially higher than market price, with a sternly worded reminder that the board and management have a fiduciary responsibility to act in the interest of shareholders. Entirely an American practice, which is now out of use because of Williams Act time extension rules (see Saturday Night Special below).

BOND: A loan in the form of an interest-paying security with a maturity date at which the full value of the loan is repaid.

CALL OPTION: An option giving the buyer the right, but not the obligation, to purchase the asset underlying the option at a specified price.

CROWN JEWELS: The most attractive assets of a company. A Crown Jewels lock-up, such as that deployed by the American company SCM in defending itself against a takeover from the British company Hanson, involves agreeing to sell these assets to a third party at a low price before the bid goes through, thus making the company much less interesting to the predator.

DAWN RAID: A practice which had a brief vogue in London in the early 1980s, whereby a predator's brokers swept into the market the instant it opened and bought up a large block of shares before the opposition had a chance to react. Robert Maxwell acquired his initial holding in British Printing with a dawn raid. The era of dawn raids didn't last long, because the institutions who sold their shares in these raids realised that, in most cases, they had done so prematurely and that the final takeover price was higher than the one they had sold out at.

DERIVATIVES: A financial contract whose value is related to – derived from – an underlying asset such as a bond, share, currency or commodity, giving the buyer control of the underlying asset. The purchase price of the derivative is usually a fraction of the value of the underlying asset. This gives the buyer leverage which may result in huge gains or huge losses.

GOLDEN PARACHUTE: A generous compensation contract awarded by management to themselves in anticipation of a takeover.

GREENMAIL: 'Green' as in money and 'mail' as in blackmail. The raider buys a significant stake in the target company in a fashion sufficiently menacing to convince it that a takeover is on the way – and might win. This may or may not be the actual intention. The target company is persuaded to buy back its own shares, usually at a high premium – and with a promise from the raider not to bid again.

HOSTILE TAKEOVER: A bid that the management of the target company doesn't like.

LEVERAGED BUY-OUT: The purchase, usually by the management, of a company, using its own assets as collateral for loans provided by banks or insurance companies.

JUNK BONDS: More technically, 'high yield' bonds or loan stock. The term 'junk' comes from the dominant high yield bond issued prior to 1978, when the market was almost entirely made up of original issue investment-grade bonds that had fallen on hard times and become more speculative – and high yielding. Only about 1,000 American corporations are judged to support so-called 'investment quality' (or A-rated) bonds as measured by Standard & Poor, Moody's or other reputable rating services, but it's unfair to describe every other company's bonds as unsafe or 'junk'. As devised by Drexel Burnham's mergers and acquisitions department in 1983, there has been in the US an explosion in mass-marketed, high-interest-yield debt securities put on the market to finance frequently hostile takeover bids. Critics fear that, in many cases, the bidders can never make the assets earn the interest on the junk bonds they have taken on – particularly if there's a downturn in the economy. For a variety of reasons, junk bonds haven't become a part of the British bid scene.

PAC-MAN DEFENCE: After the video game in which the pursued little cursor survives by attempting to gobble up his bigger enemies.

POISON PILL: A defence technique in which a company issues to its shareholders a special preferred dividend stock which is convertible, after a takeover, into the acquirer's shares; the successful bidder thus faces the prospect of heavy dilution. In a wider sense, it also applies to a defensive manoeuvre in which the target company takes on an enormous debt burden, and either distributes it to shareholders or uses it to buy up stock, thereby making itself much less attractive. Again, not used in Britain.

PROXY BATTLE: A battle between a company and some of its own shareholders. It starts with a group of dissident shareholders soliciting proxies in order to force through a shareholder resolution.

PUT OPTION: An option giving the owner the right to sell the underlying asset at a specified price.

SATURDAY NIGHT SPECIAL: A surprise tender offer with a seven- to ten-day expiration period. So called because the strategy often involves announcing it over the weekend, thus denying the rival management time to respond. Now out of use because of new state takeover laws and SEC rule changes (see SEC).

SEC — SECURITIES AND EXCHANGE COMMISSION: The US government agency that regulates securities trading. It has civil enforcement powers only, and must seek criminal prosecutions through the US Justice Department.

SCORCHED EARTH POLICY: Extreme defensive tactics by a defending company; taking on a heavy debt or selling off key assets to save itself.

SHARK REPELLENT: Special provisions in a company's charter or bylaws designed to deter bidders.

SHORT POSITION: The seller of assets he doesn't own has gone 'short'. A buyer of assets has gone 'long'.

TENDER OFFER: A cash offer to the shares of a public company for the shareholders' stock. In Britain a tender offer must be one price for 'any or all' shares, but in the US a tender offer may be made for any percentage of the outstanding stock.

WHITE KNIGHT: A friendly bidder, willing to offer more for a target's shares than an existing hostile bidder. A variation is the 'grey knight' who offers to buy the shares of the bidding company as an aid to the defence.

YUPPIE SCAM: The name given to the Wall Street insider-trading scandal after a host of smart young lawyers, bankers, brokers and arbitrageurs were found to be in a dealing ring.

——————— Greed is good ———————

Memories of the 1930s were so strong in the American psyche that, even in the 1980s, relief that one could be rich was palpable, and there was no shame in shouting it from the rooftops. As the Reagan bull market gathered pace, there were plenty of people ready to do the showing off.

When tycoon Saul Steinberg got together with another tycoon, Larry Tisch, a celebration was held at the Metropolitan Museum of Art (dubbed 'Club Met' by one journalist). 12,000 Dutch tulips (symbolic, eh?) and 50,000 French roses were on display. Tina Brown, editor of *Vanity Fair*, described the affair as a 'baronical extravagance on the scale of Castile and Aragon in the fifteenth century'.

> *If you can actually count your money then you are not really a rich man.*
>
> **J. Paul Getty**

Meanwhile, Susan Gutfreund – apparently she likes it to be pronounced 'good friend' – the wife of the head of Solomon Brothers, who were riding the bull market like no other, took it upon herself to lead this *nouvelle* society or, as Tom Wolfe described them, 'Masters of the Universe'.

She redecorated her apartment on Fifth Avenue for a reputed $20 million and booked not one but two seats on Concorde to fly a cake to Paris for her husband's 60th birthday party. After the Crash in 1987, 'Social Susie' complained: 'It's so expensive to be rich.'

Perhaps the three words that summed up the Reagan/Thatcher era were spoken by Ivan Boesky, legendary stockmarket trader and arbitrageur who finally ended up in jail. They were: 'Greed is good.' On 18 May 1986, talking to students at a California business school, Boesky said: 'Greed is all right, by the way … I think greed is healthy. You can be greedy and still feel good about yourself.' Apparently the college kids loved it, whooped with delight and no doubt looked forward to being greedy themselves.

I hope they noticed that, six months later, the Securities and Exchange Commission in New York announced that Boesky had confessed to insider trading and was cooperating with investigators.

——— Japan is buying America ———

In September 1990, a Japanese property company, Cosmo World, bought the famous Pebble Beach resort in California, with its superb golf course, for $831 million. It was a huge sum, and set off alarm bells about Japanese purchases of American assets.

> *The best investment on earth is earth.*
>
> **Louis Glickman**

In the previous decade, Japanese businessmen had become obsessed with golf. Hugely popular, golf was a crucial part of the Japanese company outing, itself an important feature of business life in Japan. There was a self-feeding escalator in becoming a member of a golf club: as the members owned the clubs, Japan's property boom of the 1980s made becoming a member a sure-fire investment. By the end of the 1980s, over twenty clubs in Japan cost more than $1 million to join, and Koganei Country Club, Tokyo's most exclusive, cost $2.7 million. There were over 1,000 under construction at the end of the 1980s, and banks were prepared to lend up to 90 per cent of the cost of membership – that membership, of course, providing the collateral.

If the 1980s provided a bull market in the USA and the UK, it was nothing compared with Japan. At the end of

1989, the Nikkei 225 Index of top Japanese companies approached 40,000, which was up 27 per cent on the year and a staggering 500 per cent on the decade. Furthermore, to add to the concern of patriotic – or should it be xenophobic? – Americans, the Japanese had bought not only Pebble Beach but the Rockefeller Center in Manhattan for over $1 billion and Columbia Pictures in Hollywood for $3.4 billion.

Needless to say (echoing the events of August 1929), the leading stockbroker, Nomura Securities, was forecasting that the Nikkei would read 80,000 by 1995. Inevitably the bubble burst, though not with a loud bang, rather with a gradual but prolonged sigh which saw the Nikkei decline throughout 1990 so that it had halved to 20,000 by September and then on to 14,309 in August 1992, a drop of over 60 per cent from its peak. Property prices in Tokyo had also fallen 60 per cent.

—— You think the bankers know —— what they're doing?

Born in Watford, the son of a plasterer, Nick Leeson enjoyed a lower-middle-class upbringing. Pushed by his mother, he worked reasonably hard at school but only gained an O-level in maths at the second attempt. He made friends easily but could be yobbish, as when he and his mates went to a disco after a football match, took their clothes off and stood on the dance floor naked. He was also beaten up by a group of strangers after a friend of his slipped his penis into the hand of a girl at the club. His friends, even his wife Lisa, often called him 'Dickhead'. Significantly, he was able to fit just as easily into the atmosphere of the City as he was into this laddish atmosphere at home.

After a spell in the back office at Morgan Stanley he joined Barings, where he helped to sort out a mess in its Singapore back office. However, Leeson wanted to be up-front on the trading floor and not in the back office, and that's where things began to go right and then very, very wrong.

To understand how Leeson brought down Barings, we have to understand why Barings was so vulnerable. Founded on Christmas Day 1762, Barings was Britain's oldest bank. By the 1980s, it was part of the British banking establishment and, as such, was conservative, patrician and risk-averse. Margaret Thatcher's successful attempt to shake up the City of London and force it to make changes in order to be competitive with the Americans and Japanese – known as Big Bang – confused Barings. However, it knew it must do something, and so it bought a small stockbroker, Henderson Grosthwaite.

As it happened, Henderson Grosthwaite employed a dealer called Christopher Heath who understood the value of Japanese warrants. These warrants were an option giving the holders the right to buy Japanese companies' shares in the future at a particular price. As the Japanese stock rose dramatically during the 1980s, the value of the warrants shot up, and Heath and his team made huge profits for Barings.

> *I shall dream about a thousand pounds tonight.
> I know I shall.*
>
> **Lewis Carroll, *Alice's Adventures
> in Wonderland***

In spite of this, the Barings hierarchy didn't really understand Heath, and never took kindly to this new star in the firmament – especially when his success made him the highest-paid man in the City by 1989. As soon as the Japanese market stopped rising and the Heath team stopped making money, Barings sacked him.

Nevertheless, Heath's legacy was a big dealing operation in the Far East, and it was into this operation that Leeson stepped and began to operate. He realised that no one at Barings' head office understood what was going on – and he took full advantage. One of the managers, reporting on Leeson, wrote: 'The general manager [Leeson] likes to be involved in the back office, and does not regard it as an undue burden.'

In other words, Leeson could do what he liked, and he could also cover up any mistakes. And in the dealing world of the markets, mistakes could be big and expensive. Mistakes were made by the dealers every day; either they were counter-balanced by successful deals or – and this is the key in Leeson's case – they were put into what was known as the 88888 error account. All banks have such accounts to handle discrepancies which can be sorted out later. However, the sums involved are never massive. In Leeson's case, because no one was checking (they didn't really want to check, because their bonuses depended on the massive profits Leeson was supposed to be making), he was putting all his expensive mistakes into the 88888 account. In his first year of operation, Leeson made losses of £2 million, but no one at Barings knew. Indeed, they began to treat him as their star trader, telling him to buy the Japanese Nikkei 225 Index as part of an arbitrage strategy. He did so, and lied about his dealing, telling his bosses he was buying at a lower price than he had and selling at a higher price than he had. His bosses believed him, lionising him as the 'turbo arbitrageur'. As Leeson was bankrupting Barings, Peter Baring told the Bank of England in one of their chats over tea (which is what passed as regulation by the Bank): 'The recovery in profitability has been amazing, leaving Barings to conclude that it was not acutely very difficult to make money in the securities business.'

What was Leeson supposed to be doing? He was supposed to be arbitraging the Nikkei 225 between Singapore and Osaka. When very small price differences opened up between the two markets, he was supposed to exploit it by buying where the contract was cheaper and selling where it was more expensive. Each trade had a balancing purchase and sale, and therefore carried no risk. The profits on each trade were small, but if enough trades were carried out they could mount up nicely.

> *When as a young man I started to be successful I was referred to as a gambler. My operations increased in scope and volume. Then I was known as a speculator. The sphere of my activities continued to expand and presently I was known as a banker. Actually I had been doing the same thing all the time.*
>
> **Sir Ernest Cassel**

Unfortunately, Leeson found this far too boring. He was the turbo arbitrageur, wasn't he? He would take big punts without a countervailing, balancing trade, and he would win big. Except that he didn't win. By the end of 1993, he had lost £25 million but still his bosses didn't know, because he had hidden his losses in the 88888 account. To balance the losses, he sold options for which people paid £30 million in premiums. This was extremely risky. If the options went the wrong way, he stood to lose hundreds of millions of pounds.

During 1994 he pursued what's known as a 'straddle' strategy, whereby he sold both call and put options (if you think the market's going up, you buy a call option; if down, a put option) on the Nikkei. For this to succeed, he needed the Nikkei to remain stable. In that case, neither the call nor the put options which people had bought would be worth exercising, the option would run out of time and Leeson would keep the premium.

While this was going on, he presented fake figures which showed that profits from his operations in 1994 were £20 million, or 20 per cent of Barings' entire profit. No wonder the gullible at head office wanted to believe. Think what he was doing for their bonuses. Nevertheless, Barings sent their internal auditor, James Baker, to check his figures. He failed to find the massive option deals hidden in 88888, and even recommended that Barings make every effort to ensure that Leeson wasn't poached by a competitor.

By the end of 1994, Leeson was in big trouble. He had $270 million in futures losses, balanced by only $220 million in premium income from the potentially dangerous options sales. To make up the $59 million shortfall, he forged a $50 million payment supposedly from a US broker, Spear, Leeds and Kellogg. Almost unbelievably, neither Barings nor Coopers and Lybrand, their auditors, noticed that the confirming fax from the US broker had 'From Nick & Lisa' at the top. In other words, Leeson had sent it from his home. When bankers and accountants *want* to believe that something is true, they don't bother with pieces of paper that tell them what they are looking at *cannot* be true.

In a wonderful irony, Barings paid Leeson a Christmas bonus of £450,000 in 1994 for a year's work in which he had put a time bomb under their bank. On 17 January 1995 the bomb went off, not in London or Singapore, but in the Japanese city of Kobe, where an earthquake measuring 7.2 on the Richter scale destroyed the city. The Nikkei plunged, exposing Leeson's positions, and he lost £100 million in a few days. Those who had bought put options were set to gain massively. To try to offset these gains, he needed the Nikkei to recover, and to achieve this Leeson started to buy Nikkei 225. This was the final madness. No single individual can influence a market as big as the Japanese stockmarket.

> **'What's one and one and one and one and one and one and one and one and one and one?'**
> **'I don't know', said Alice. 'I lost count.'**
>
> **Lewis Carroll,**
> **Through the Looking-Glass**

Of course, Leeson was doing what every gambler can to make sure he doesn't lose. He was doubling up. This strategy works as long as your capital is limitless. In the end you will win a bet and, as you have doubled up each time, by definition it will eradicate your losses. But Barings' resources were not limitless. He carried on losing, and demanded more cash from Barings in London. Incredibly, they sent him an amount that was twice as much as their own capital, apparently believing that he was dealing on behalf of clients and that they didn't stand to lose the money.

On his last day, 23 February 1995, Leeson lost £144 million. By this time he knew the game was up, and he ran. A friend drove him and his wife to the airport, and he fled first to Kuala Lumpur and then to Borneo. They were finally arrested at Frankfurt airport on their way back to London. He was extradited to Singapore and given a long jail sentence.

And what of Barings? They knew they were in serious trouble once the scale of Leeson's losses began to unfold, but they were confident that the City would rally round; someone would buy them, and life would continue much as before. One of the first banks they approached was the huge American firm, Morgan Stanley. This was how a Morgan Stanley executive recalled the first meeting with Peter Baring, the chairman, and Peter Norris, the head of investment banking and the man responsible for Leeson: 'It was pathetic. Peter Baring kept a stiff upper lip but looked as though he was choking back tears. He was obviously in a state of shock. He said that three days earlier he had been preparing to announce record profits for 1994; then, forty eight hours ago, he had learned that his bank was bust; and now he was offering to sell it to us for one pound sterling. Norris, on the other hand, behaved as though the whole meeting was a waste of time. He just sat there sulking, not saying much, not being much help. It was the most astonishing display of arrogance. He knew the bank was bust, but seemed to think he could sort the whole thing out by himself.'

Morgan Stanley declined to buy, even at £1, and so did every other leading bank in London, even after

Eddie George, Governor of the Bank of England, hastily summoned back from his skiing holiday, called them all together to find a solution. No one was prepared to step forward, especially when Barings told them that they couldn't be certain how big their losses on Leeson's futures position would be. But they certainly needed $650 million immediately. Furthermore, Barings still expected to be allowed to pay $95 million in bonuses to their staff, and the family didn't expect to have their holdings in the bank diluted.

The Bank put them into administration, a form of bankruptcy.

> *The different branches of arithmetic – Ambition, Distraction, Uglification and Derision.*
>
> **Lewis Carroll, *Alice's Adventures in Wonderland***

—— Options – what are they, and —— who started them?

We can't be sure who started options, but this is a story told by Aristotle about options which were put in place by the philosopher, Thales of Miletus.

Thales became fed up with his friends chastising him about being a philosopher. Philosophy was a waste of time, they said, because it didn't make any money. Nevertheless, he would show them he could make money. As well as being a philosopher, Thales was a gifted meteorologist. Predicting a good olive harvest for the following year, he offered the olive-press owners a down payment for letting him use, *if he wanted to*, their presses the next year at a certain price. In other words, he took out an option – but, importantly, he didn't need to take it up. However, his prediction was correct, there was a bumper olive harvest, presses were in great demand and he was able to charge them out at much higher prices than the prices he had negotiated. He made a lot of money and achieved a classic and successful option, an exercise that is carried out by the million every day in the trading markets of the world.

—— Is your bank manager your —— best friend?

We all make mistakes, and usually we pay for them. Your bank makes mistakes and, again, you pay for them.

Take loans to Latin American countries in the 1980s, which were made presumably on the basis that people and companies go bust but countries do not. Maybe they don't, but they can certainly refuse to repay loans, or even to pay interest. That's precisely what happened, and all the banks kept quiet until the American firm Citicorp came clean about its loans to Latin America and wrote them off completely. That forced the British banks to come clean as well, and in 1987 they made provisions against bad debts in developing countries as follows:

Lloyds	£1.066 billion
Midland (since bought by HSBC)	£1.016 billion
Barclays	£713 million
NatWest	£610 million
Total	**£3.405 billion**

Actually, this wildly understated the true situation. The provision was only about a third of the debt, i.e. the banks were saying that 67 per cent of the debt was good, whereas Third World debt was being traded at 25–30 per cent of its face value. Therefore the provision, to be realistic, should have been 75 per cent, in which case the banks should have been writing off not £3.4 billion but more like £8 billion.

> **When Will Sutton was asked why he robbed banks, he replied: 'Because that's where the money is.'**

It's a pity that home-grown entrepreneurs don't receive the same support. At the beginning of the 1980s, Anita Roddick wanted to borrow £5,000 to start her own company, Body Shop. Her bank manager refused to lend it to her. Fortunately, a local garage-owner did so, and five years later when Body Shop floated on the stock-market, that £5,000 became £13.5 million. By the end of 1988 it was £30 million.

And who pays for these wild loans to South America and for missed opportunities in West Sussex? You do:

1. You are charged 3, maybe 4, even 5 per cent over base rate for your overdraft.
2. You pay a percentage fee for arranging the overdraft facility.
3. You pay a fee every time you bank a cheque.
4. You pay a fee every time you write a cheque.
5. You pay penalties if you exceed your overdraft limit.

> *A banker is a fellow who lends you his umbrella when the sun is shining and wants it back the minute it begins to rain.*
>
> **Mark Twain**

It can get worse. A few years ago, Lloyds split their customers into four groups and imposed charges according to the service they would receive, which ranged from virtually nothing to having your local manager in for a chat. The other banks couldn't believe their luck as Lloyd's customers departed in their droves. Lloyds have dropped the scheme.

> *If you owe the bank $100 that's your problem. If you owe the bank $100 million that's the bank's problem.*
>
> **J. Paul Getty**

—— Dam-busting bombs don't —— come cheap

Since the Second World War it has always been a source of disquiet in Britain that non-wealth-creators, i.e. solicitors, accountants, estate agents and their ilk, are rewarded far more highly than wealth-creators such as engineers. Perhaps this accounts for Britain's decline as a manufacturing nation.

Before the war, engineering companies paid well for their best engineers. For example, Barnes Wallis, whose achievements included design of the Wellesley and Wellington bombers (incorporating his innovative geodetic design) and, more famously, the development of his dam-busting bomb, was paid £2,500 per annum by Vickers in the early 1930s (£137,500). At the same time, he bought a four-bedroom house overlooking Effingham golf course in Surrey for £2,500. I'm sure everyone today would like to be paid what their house cost.

Later in the 1930s, Rolls-Royce lured Stanley Hooker away from the Admiralty for a salary of £1,000 (£55,000). Not many people of 30 were earning £1,000 in the 1930s.

More worrying is whether we are creating a dangerously lop-sided or even unfair society. Frank Welsh, in his admirable book *Uneasy City*, quoted Ben Jonson, 'but these same citizens, they are such sharks', and went on to write: 'That so many of our brightest young people (and, according to the Cambridge University Appointments Board, many of them are among the more academically successful) can seek no finer end than to be bookkeepers is disturbing enough, but the consequences are even more so. The role of the accountant in industry is admittedly always necessary and sometimes important, but it is essentially negative. Companies may avoid bankruptcy by the skill of their accountants, but they do not become successful thereby. It is the engineers, the scientists and the salesmen who generate growth.'

The *Guardian* at the end of 2005 agreed: '[The City of] London is now a highly successful world centre, claiming the lion's share of international financial markets ... The unacceptable face of this success is the ludicrously disproportionate reward for activities that come way down anyone's scale of genuine social usefulness compared with medicine, nursing, teaching, manufacturing and a host of other activities ... If any of the major [political] parties is looking for a new sense of purpose the pursuit of fairness should infuse everything they plan. Fairness does not mean equality. Nor does it mean confiscation. It simply means turning policies now to reverse the winner-takes-all mentality that, if left unchecked, could turn Britain into a much less harmonious society than it is now.'

> *We live in a society that rewards City spivs and lawyers, car fleet managers and advertising touts more than scientists and teachers.*
>
> **Richard Dawkins**

The best definition of an accountant/finance director I have encountered came when the chairman of a successful Yorkshire manufacturing business said something at the Annual General Meeting with which his finance director didn't agree. When the accountant stood up to interject, the chairman waved him down, saying: 'Nay lad, sit thee down, tha's just the scorer.'

The Royal Family – the damnedest millstone

In the early 1800s, the exact income of the Royal Family wasn't revealed, although reformers felt 'there could be little doubt the King was the richest individual in Europe, perhaps in the whole world'.

In 1817, Parliament voted an extra £500,000 (£55 million today) above his customary income for the use of the King and the Prince Regent, of which over £20,000 (£2.2 million) was spent on snuff-boxes.

The Duke of Wellington described them as 'the damnedest millstones about the neck of any government that can be imagined'.

───── The Queen has never won ───── the Derby

At the end of the 1980s, in his book *Britain's 400 Richest People*, Philip Beresford estimated that the Queen was worth £6,700 million: 'The richest woman in the world, the Queen's wealth stems from two fortunes. There are the Crown Estates, which contain much of her 267,000 acres of land, including 350 valuable acres of central London. She also owns virtually all the land around the coast of Britain, between the high- and low-water marks. This gives her the rights to land when it is reclaimed and any mineral rights, giving an annual income of £2 million a year.'

'All these assets of the Crown Estates were valued at £1,200 million in March 1987. But the Queen is really the custodian of these estates, rather than the direct beneficiary. She pays all the revenues to the Treasury (£29.4 million in 1987) in return for an annual payment from the Civil List. In 1990 the Queen received £5.09 million.'

'The Queen's second fortune, which is more clearly her own property, is hers to sell if she wishes, although this is thought to be a very unlikely eventuality. This fortune embraces the royal treasures such as an art collection, with works by all the Dutch and Italian masters, and several hundred drawings by Leonardo da

Vinci. It also includes the royal antiques, which require a 75-volume catalogue to cover them all. The royal stamp collection, started by George V, runs over 330 albums. The Queen's jewel collection includes over 20 tiaras.'

'In addition, racing stables, stud farms and property in Britain (50,000 acres at Balmoral and 20,000 acres at Sandringham) are held by the Queen personally. There are also valuable properties on the continent and in America, though these are shrouded in secrecy. The total value of this portfolio has been estimated at nearly £3 billion.'

'The Queen has stocks and shares in an equity portfolio which is managed with utter discretion by blue chip banks and brokers in the City. This was valued after the 1987 crash at around £1.9 billion, but it increased in value by some 25 per cent in line with the surge in world stock markets in 1988 and 1989.'

—— Your Majesty – you've shopped —— and you've dropped

According to the authoritative *Sunday Times* Rich List published each year, Her Majesty Queen Elizabeth has had a very rough ride since 1989. In that year, the List put her as *the* richest person in Britain with a fortune of £5.2 billion (about £8 billion today). I don't know what she did with all that money, but by 2005 the List had relegated her to 180th, with only £270 million.

Robert Maxwell

When he was at the height of his powers in the late 1980s, Robert Maxwell said he wouldn't leave a penny to his children. This was a surprise to most, as it was well known that the Maxwells were a close-knit family. However, Maxwell, a former Labour Member of Parliament, explained that he was opposed in principle to inherited wealth, saying: 'It can stifle initiative in a later generation.'

In 1991, when he threw himself off the back of his yacht to drown in the Mediterranean, the *Sunday Times* Rich List quoted him as the eighth richest man in England, with a fortune of £1.2 billion. He had his wish of not leaving anything to his children granted.

Kevin, when questioned about his father's decision not to leave him any money, said to William Davis, author of *Children of the Rich*: 'I am grateful for his decision. I do not believe that a child has an inalienable right to inherit. I am very comfortable that I have to fend for myself and may do well through my own endeavours. I have no God-given right to be a billionaire just because Dad is. I went to school with children of wealthy parents, and I saw how much unhappiness can be caused if one has a lot of money at an early age. Some of them had drug problems. I am also glad that money isn't an issue in our family; if it were, we might so easily end up quarrelling.'

Ironically, in 1995 Kevin Maxwell made it into the *Guinness Book of Records* as the world's biggest bankrupt, with debts of £406.8 million.

Members of Parliament at £400 — a year? Far too much

Members of the House of Commons have been paid a salary and travelling expenses since 1911. Before that, if you had to be paid you weren't considered fit to govern the country.

From 1911 to 1937 they were paid £400 a year, the equivalent today initially of £44,000. However, allowing for the inflation brought on by the First World War, in the 1920s and 30s it was worth about £22,000 in today's money. In 1937 they received a 50 per cent increase to £600, or about £33,000 in today's terms. In 1947 they received another raise to £1,000 but, following the inflationary Second World War, they were still worse off than in the late 1930s. In 1957 that £1,000 was raised to £1,750, which was an improvement, and in 1964 to £3,250 – a considerable improvement, though it's still only the equivalent of about £65,000 today. 1972 brought another rise to £4,500, which barely kept pace with inflation, and 1975 a rise to £5,750, which certainly didn't keep pace with the rampant inflation of the mid-1970s. 1976 brought a small rise (under the inflationary circumstances) to £6,062, followed by further rises to £6,270 in 1977, £6,897 in 1978, and £9,450 in 1979. (This 37 per cent rise was seen as provocative when the government was trying to tell the trades unions that large wage increases were self-defeating.) Undeterred, MPs voted themselves a further 13.5 per cent rise to £10,725 in 1980 and a 30 per cent rise to £13,950 in 1981.

Many people today think MPs are on the make. Indeed, one of the reasons put forward for the Tories' defeat in the 1997 general election was that many felt that they were in it for the money. Whether or not most people think Members of Parliament are overpaid, this is what they were actually paid in 2004: £57,485.

In 1969, they were also granted an allowance for secretarial and research expenses, and from April 2004, MPs received an Incidental Expenses Provision of £19,325 and a staffing allowance of between £66,458 and £77,354.

Since 1972, MPs have been able to claim reimbursement for the additional cost of staying overnight away from their main residence while on parliamentary business. This is known as the Additional Costs Allowance, and from April 2004 it has been £20,902 per year.

Ministerial salaries as from 1 April 2004 – in addition to their £57,485 pay as Members of the House of Commons – are:

Prime Minister	£121,437
Cabinet Minister (Commons)	£72,862
Cabinet Minister (Lords)	£98,899
Minister of State (Commons)	£37,796
Minister of State (Lords)	£77,220
Parliamentary Under Secretary (Commons)	£28,688
Parliamentary Under Secretary (Lords)	£67,255

These ministers weren't as successful as their predecessors in pre-Victorian times. Bribes and commissions would yield about £10,000 (over £1 million) a year to anyone in government. Some did much better – for example, John Scott, 1st Earl of Eldon and Lord Chancellor for 25 years until his death in 1838. He was the son of a Newcastle coal merchant but he left a fortune of £707,000 (about £80 million). In 1830, the

Duke of Wellington, as Prime Minister, was paid £4,000 plus a pension of £13,000, i.e. a total of £17,000, the equivalent of £1.87 million today.

Nor was the corruption confined to MPs. John Moore, Archbishop of Canterbury, left £1 million (£110,000 million) when he died in 1805 after a career of clever exploitation of Church posts and estates.

—— The rising price of Eton ——

In 1870, it was usual, on leaving Eton, to place £10 inconspicuously somewhere in the headmaster's study, 'as with one's medical adviser'.

In 1896, the school fee was £8 8s a term, i.e. 8 guineas (£924 in today's money), and the payment for boarding in a house was £110 a year (£12,100 today).

In 1909, school fees had risen to £10 10s a term and house payments to £115 10s a year.

In 1925, the all-in annual charge was £230 (£12,650 in today's money), where it remained into the 1930s.

By 1949, the fees were £308 a year (£9,240 today), plus a £10 games subscription (another £300).

By 1957, the figures had risen to £400 (£10,000) for fees, £13 for games.

By 1967, the overall cost of keeping a boy at Eton was officially £595 (£11,900) a year.

And in 1970 further increases were announced, raising the total to £765 (£12,240), which, by a happy coincidence, is almost exactly in line with the 1896–1970 decline in the value of money.

However, after 1970 the rise in fees at public (i.e. private) schools really got into its stride, with the annual charge at Eton reaching £11,934 in 1995 and then doubling to £23,688 in 2005. In other words, they doubled in a decade of historically low inflation. This excited the Office of Fair Trading (OFT), which found 50 of the country's leading private schools guilty of running an illegal price-fixing cartel, after exchanging detailed financial information.

The prices charged were remarkably similar:

	1995	2005
Charterhouse	£11,910	£23,955
Eton	£11,930	£23,688
Harrow	£12,630	£23,625
Winchester	£12,270	£25,500

The OFT said: 'This systematic exchange of confidential information as to intended fee increases was anti-competitive and resulted in parents being charged higher fees than would otherwise be the case.'

Interestingly, the OFT investigation was reportedly prompted by a student hacking into his school's financial records.

It would seem that if there was one group of people in the country capable of looking after themselves without help from the government, it was those that could afford private school fees.

——— India must be plundered ———

In the 18th and 19th centuries, assets of £500,000 (£55 million) would place a man among the richest in the country.

Banks and industrial companies didn't generate the

fortunes of today. However, plundering India was lucrative – Robert Clive, the venerated 'Clive of India', went to India a penniless clerk and returned in 1760 with £317,000 (£35 million) in precious stones and securities. When he went back to Bengal in 1765, on a mission to root out corruption, he returned with another £165,000 (£18 million). When Parliament accused Clive of enriching himself, he replied: 'By God, Chairman, at this moment I stand astounded at my own moderation.'

Inherited wealth

Malcolm Forbes built his father's business magazine – *Forbes* – into a millionaire's house journal. It gave him an annual income of $10 million and he lives up to it, with eight houses around the world and a huge yacht.

When people ask him how he became so rich, he says: 'Industry and ability, you spell those words I-n-h-e-r-i-t-a-n-c-e.'

Indeed, the best way to get rich is to have a rich Dad. When the *Sunday Times* published its first Rich List in 1989, the editor, Andrew Neil, was apparently appalled to find that over half the people on the List had inherited wealth. The 1990s will have been more reassuring for him, as the self-made millionaires caught up with and passed the inheritors.

Property has made many very rich, largely because of the gearing effect. The property dealer borrows most of his purchase price; the total rises 20 per cent, but his stake, if he has borrowed ten times his initial stake, rises by 200 per cent. (The same applies, of course, to all the people who have bought houses in the past 60 years.)

However, real fortunes have also been made by great inventors who exploited their inventions skilfully. James Dyson made sure that his second invention, the bagless vacuum cleaner, made a fortune for him, after his first, the wheelbarrow with a ball rather than a wheel, made one for others after he sold the idea for £10,000.

As the country has grown more prosperous, great wealth has been accumulated by those who have exploited the manufacture and distribution of food and drink – the Vesteys, Westons, Sainsburys, Guinnesses. Leisure activities have enriched operators of cut-price holidays and airlines. Popular music has put no fewer than 48 pop-star millionaires in the *Sunday Times* Rich List.

> *Of the billionaires I have known, money just brings out the basic traits in them. If they were jerks before they had money, they are simply jerks with a billion dollars.*
>
> **Warren Buffett**

The Super Rich

According to the *Sunday Times* Rich List, these are the 'Super Rich'. Number two in 1989 was the Duke of Westminster with £3.2 billion, and he seems to have done OK because in 2005 he still had £5.2 billion, which was just ahead of the rise in prices. Mind you, he was down to third place behind two people that no one in Britain had ever heard of in 1989 – Lakshmi Mittal, with

£14.8 billion made from that 19th-century smokestack industry, steel; and the Russian, Roman Abramovich, with £7.5 billion made from that quintessential 20th-century industry, oil.

> **Lack of money is the root of all evil.**
>
> **George Bernard Shaw**

If Abramovich has put his £7.5 billion on deposit at, say, 5 per cent, it would earn him £375 million a year, enough to buy thirteen Rio Ferdinands. God, one's enough.

Very durable were the Rausing family at fourth both in 1989 and 2005, with £1.9 billion turning into £4.95 billion. They made their fortune with Tetrapak packaging, which always amazes me because I can never open their milk and fruit juice cartons. Perhaps that's why I'm not on the List, even though it now stretches to 1,000 people.

> **There are two times in a man's life when he should not speculate: when he can't afford it and when he can.**
>
> **Mark Twain**

A number of those on the 1989 List found their collars fingered subsequently, either by the tax authorities (Octav Botnar, supposedly with a fortune of £1 billion, who handled Nissan cars in Britain) or by the police (Robert Maxwell with £675 million, or rather his son after he had jumped off his boat). Gerald Ronson, apparently the country's twelfth richest man with £500 million in 1989, enjoyed a spell at Her Majesty's pleasure following conviction for his involvement in the Guinness scandal. Up at 37th in 1989 was Asil Nadir with £192 million. He too was forced to flee the country, wanted for dubious practices at his company, Polly Peck.

Jim Slater, the legendary stockmarket guru and 'asset-stripper' par excellence of the late 1960s and early 70s, was back with £50 million after crashing, along with many others, in the oil-price-rise-induced financial crisis of the mid-1970s. He proudly announced then that he had become a 'minus-millionaire' with debts of over £1 million.

> *It's better, I think, not to remember how much money you have, so you still have to work hard.*
>
> **Y.K. Pao**

Owen Oyston, joint 184th with a mere £33 million, was another who failed to convince the authorities that his predatory activities were in the best interests of humanity.

A spell in clink doesn't necessarily impoverish people. Jeffrey Archer, the bullshitting and boorish perjurer, was still rated the 751st richest man in Britain in 2005, with £65 million. I haven't noticed that it's endeared him to anyone.

> *Just as I'm five times as rich as you are, and five times as clever.*
>
> **Lewis Carroll,**
> ***Through the Looking-Glass***

Of course, after a decade of general prosperity (especially for the already rich), and after a further fifteen years of inflation, the £30 million which got you into the top 200 in 1989 didn't get you near the top 1,000 in 2005. Even £50 million, which would have placed you at joint 116th in 1989, put you at joint 938th in 2005. A bad day on the markets that knocked you to £49.5 million and you'd be out of the top 1,000.

Alan Sugar, the likeable self-made man who now tells us all how to make a bob or two in the rough and ready world of business, was fifteenth in 1989 with £432 million and is still up there, but his current £760 million has relegated him to 55th.

The secretive Barclay brothers – who are now quite high profile thanks to their ownership of newspapers, especially the *Daily Telegraph* – are serious players with £1.2 billion, which puts them at 33rd equal. Their more modest £250 million in 1989 was ranked higher at 27th. £1.2 billion then would have put them joint seventh with John Paul Getty II and the Vesteys.

Richard Branson, though only 38 years old in 1989, had already made £125 million, which put him joint 51st with Sir John Baring and family. By 2005, Branson had increased his fortune to a fabulous £3 billion, which made him the seventh richest person in Britain. The Barings didn't make the top 1,000 after one of their employees, Nick Leeson, lost them their bank and all their money.

I'm not a paranoid, deranged millionaire. Goddamit, I'm a billionaire!

Howard Hughes

Our grandfathers would have been staggered (after all, the *maximum* wage for a footballer in 1950 was £10 per week), but at 654th equal in 2005, David Beckham and his wife Posh were apparently worth £75 million.

In spite of his ability to spend money, Elton John displayed an even greater ability to accumulate, and had moved his fortune up from £40 million in 1989 to £185 million in 2005.

In book publishing we should raise a cheer for J.K. Rowling, author of the *Harry Potter* books. We can confidently say that no one outside her immediate circle had heard of her in 1989. By 2005, her royalties had made her worth £500 million and put her at 96th equal. We can also confidently say that she will almost certainly reach the magic £1 billion.

Aristotle Onassis never wore an overcoat. Why? Because if he wore a coat he would have to give a big tip to the cloakroom girl. And the coat would have to be expensive because rich people are expected to wear expensive clothes. Finally, he would have to insure it in case someone stole it. 'Without an overcoat I save $20,000 a year.'

Traditionally, Labour governments have made life hard for the rich. After all, the Labour Party was formed just over 100 years ago with the express object of distributing wealth more evenly, essentially by taking it from the rich and giving it to the poor. It's perhaps surprising, then, that the wealthy have never had it so good as they have in the eight years of Tony Blair's Labour governments. As

Phillip Beresford points out in his *Rich List 2005*: 'Just eight years ago when Tony Blair came to power, the wealth of the richest 1,000 [people in Britain] stood at £98.99 billion. The top ten alone in this year's list are worth £52.55 billion – £10 billion more than the top 200 put together 10 years ago.'

—— The most expensive meal —— per head

The *Guinness Book of Records* quotes the most expensive meal per head as follows:

'On 5 July 2001, six diners at Pétrus, London, UK, spent £44,007 ($61,941) on one meal. The bill consisted mainly of five bottles of wine as, once the bill had been added up, the £300 charge for food was taken off. The most expensive bottle was a 1947 Château Pétrus vintage claret worth £12,300, followed by the slightly cheaper 1945 Château Pétrus at £11,600. A 1946 Château Pétrus cost £9,400, apparently due to this year being a poor year. A 1900 Château d'Yquem dessert wine cost £9,200 and a 1982 bottle of Montrachet was a snip at £1,400. The remaining £107 consisted of water, a fruit juice, cigarettes and six glasses of champagne.'

In the good old days of executive dining rooms in companies, the cost of each lunch, when all the back-up staff were taken into consideration, was quite hefty. I remember when I was writing the company history of United Biscuits, the company secretary told me that my lunch with the chairman, Sir Hector Laing, had cost over £100. Every lunch in that dining room cost over £100 once all the costs were taken into account.

Mind you, it was well worth it because one of the other diners reminded Sir Hector of a heated discussion (Hector liked heated discussions, especially after a drink or two) he had had with the Prime Minister, Margaret Thatcher, then in her all-powerful prime, when she was staying on Sir Hector's estate in the north of Scotland. He got so annoyed that he stormed out, leapt into his private aeroplane and proceeded to buzz the house. It then became so dark that he couldn't see his own landing strip, and had to be talked down into the local RAF station.

—— A peerage, sir? That'll be just —— £150,000 (£7.5 million) to you

Lloyd George, successful Liberal Prime Minister during the First World War, had put together a coalition but, once the war was over, he worried that he might be isolated. To fund his electoral machine, he found the sale of honours a very fruitful source of revenue.

A peerage would cost at least £150,000 (£7.5 million), a hereditary knighthood £80,000 (£4 million). A single knighthood was cheap at just £12,000 (£600,000). This was all too good to be true, and Lloyd George invented a new gong, the Order of the British Empire or OBE. These were dead cheap, and he awarded over 250,000. Because of the many dubious characters who paid for one, it was openly referred to as the 'Order of the Bad Egg'.

> *The man who gets ahead in business is the man who knows what he wants – and what he is willing to give up to get.*
>
> **Lord Beaverbrook**

—— Beware those clever bankers ——

Arnold (later Lord) Weinstock was the son of a Jewish tailor who arrived in Britain from Poland in 1906. After serving in the British forces in the Second World War, Weinstock worked for an estate agent in London's West End. He married Netta Sobell, daughter of Sir Michael Sobell, the founder of Radio and Allied Industries. Arnold joined his father-in-law's company and built it up during the 1950s to such an extent that it was able to take over the much larger GEC in the early 1960s. Later he took over AEI and English Electric to become Britain's largest electrical engineering company.

By the time of the dotcom boom in the late 1990s, GEC was vast and Weinstock's shares were valued at £500 million. His approach to business had always been relatively cautious and GEC had always held a huge cash mountain. When he retired, his successors, notably chairman George Simpson, allowed investment banks in the City to persuade them to buy the supposed growth companies of the future. Mesmerised by these dotcom companies, GEC bought two and used cash instead of their own shares. The companies proved to be worthless, and pretty soon so was GEC. It renamed itself Marconi but that didn't save it, and the rump was recently sold to

Ericsson. Weinstock died a broken man with his £500 million worth of GEC shares worth virtually nothing.

> *Sometimes I lie awake at night and ask, 'Where have I gone wrong?' Then a voice says to me, 'This is going to take more than one night.'*
>
> **Charlie Brown**

—— Luxuries become necessities ——

When new items are invented, their low volumes and lengthy manufacturing processes mean that they are expensive and only the wealthy can afford them. As the volume increases the price falls, leading to greater volumes and even lower prices, and so on. One way of measuring how prices have fallen is to calculate how many hours the average working person has to labour to pay for these former luxuries, now deemed essentials.

Product	Early cost (hours of labour) and year	1970 cost (hours of labour)	2000 cost (hours of labour)
Motor car	4,696 hours in 1908	1,397	1,350
Refrigerator	3,162 hours in 1915	112	60
Long-distance phone call	90 hours in 1915	0.4	0.03
Air travel (1,000 miles)	221 hours in 1919	18	10
Microwave oven	2,467 hours in 1947	176	14
Colour television	562 hours in 1954	174	20

> *In our modern economy it seems unlikely that the middle-class morality about money will be able to survive. I, for example, was brought up never to buy anything until I had the cash to pay for it. If everyone did the same, i.e. bought nothing on credit, our economy would go smash.*
>
> **W.H. Auden, 1970**

——— Don't think a 'pre-nup' will ——— protect you

In 2000, a ground-breaking judgement was handed down in a divorce case which has caused great consternation to Britain's rich men.

Alan Miller, a wealthy hedge fund manager, was married for less than three years to Melissa, who worked for a pharmaceutical company in Cambridge and lived in a one-bedroom rented flat. The divorce cost him £4,935.83 *a day*, i.e. £5 million. In his view, the award was outrageous: 'She worked for half of the marriage and had a relaxing time for the other half, spending much of her time shopping for the house I bought in France. You know, her email address starts off with "Must-do-lunch Melissa". And she's never bothered changing it.'

> *One of the difficult tasks of this world is to convince a woman that even a bargain costs money.*
>
> **Edgar Watson Hose**

Other women have been projected into the Rich List by their divorce settlements, for example Alisa Marks, wife of French Connection (FCUK) boss Stephen Marks. She was awarded £36.5 million. Sally Croker-Poole was awarded £20 million in her divorce from the Aga Khan. Lady Conran should have held on for a little longer. When she divorced Sir Terence, she was awarded only £10.5 million – a mere 13 per cent of his estimated £80-million fortune. This was dwarfed by the £100 million paid to his wife Joy by Peter Harrison, the computer tycoon. Sir Martin Sorrell, boss of the advertising agency giant WPP, paid his wife Sandra £30 million, a sum she apparently regarded as too little.

Probably the world record for divorce pay-outs has been achieved by Ron Perelman, who has divorced four times. At the first one in 1984 he agreed to pay Faith Golding $8 million ($4.5m or £18m in today's money); in the second one in 1994 he paid Claudia Cohen a whopping $80 million ($45m or £67m); in number three in 1998 he paid Patricia Duff $30 million ($15m or £24m); and finally in 2006 he is paying Ellen Barkin $20 million. Throw in the legal costs and adjust for inflation, and his wandering eye has cost him so far about $250m, or £140m. He can afford it. Last, year, *Forbes* magazine estimated his fortune at $6 billion, making him the 34th richest man in the USA.

> *There are three faithful friends – an old wife, an old dog and ready money.*

Benjamin Franklin

And how have the lawyers been faring? As you would expect, they have been doing very nicely, thank you. However, even a lawyer can be hoist by his own petard. When corporate lawyer Charles Ashton left his wife, he was forced to give her a 50 per cent share of the joint family assets. He expected this, but what he didn't expect was the judgement that he must pay about 50 per cent of his substantial after-tax income of £270,000 for the rest of his working life. He commented: 'I feel as if I've been given a life sentence.'

And men – and women (remember Nicola Horlick) – don't think that a pre-nuptial agreement limiting your liabilities will necessarily save you. The courts aren't obliged to take them into account. No wonder marriage is a threatened institution.

> *Keep looking tanned, live in an elegant building (even if you're in the cellar), be seen in smart restaurants (even if you nurse one drink) and if you borrow, borrow big.*
>
> **Aristotle Onassis**

The erection index

In bull markets, some investors get horny and show a determination to build the largest erection in town.

In New York in 1929, the year of the Crash, Walter Chrysler erected the Chrysler Building, higher than any previous skyscraper. In the City of London in the early 1970s, the National Westminster Bank built the

NatWest Tower (ironically, when the 1973–5 crash came, NatWest had to quash the rumour that they were going bust). The Petronas Towers in Kuala Lumpur were completed in 1997, just before the onset of the Asian financial crisis.

The lesson – when a new record is set for an erection, *sell*.

> **The big difference between sex for money and sex for free is that sex for money costs less.**
>
> **Brendon Francis**

Talking of erections, did you know that the American drug company Pfizer, which is making millions of dollars from Viagra, is thinking of erecting a statue to the woman chemist who appreciated the potential of the drug, and who died recently? She was researching ways of stimulating the heart for those suffering a heart attack. She found the answer, Viagra. Then, using her imagination, she thought: 'If it stimulates the heart, what else might it stimulate?'

Far more people suffer from impotence than have heart attacks.

Give it away

Francis Bacon, that great 17th-century lawyer, philosopher and master of the English language, said of money: 'It's like muck, not good except to be spread.'

> *Any man who has $10,000 left when he dies is a failure.*
>
> **Errol Flynn**

One of John D. Rockefeller's advisers said to him: 'You must give it away. It is rolling up like an avalanche that will crush you and your children and your children's children.'

Andrew Carnegie made hundreds of millions (billions in today's money) and gave most of it away, saying: 'The man who dies rich dies disgraced.'

> *It is better to give than to lend and it costs about the same.*
>
> **Philip Gibbs**

Affluenza

Sudden wealth syndrome, otherwise known as affluenza, has hit many of the newly rich, whether from the dotcom boom or the entertainment and sports world.

Mark McCormack dealt with rich people initially in golf, then in sport generally, and finally in many walks of life. His view on sports stars was that many couldn't cope with two problems – when to retire and what to do next. On retirement, he said: 'Towards the end of their career, sports stars are more mature and receptive to advice. But it is an emotional time and many leave it too long.'

On their over-confidence in the chosen second career, he said: 'They think because they were good at sport, to start a restaurant or a magazine will be a piece of cake. Ninety-nine per cent of the time they get killed because of that super-confidence.'

———————— **Blow his tits off** ————————

In the Reagan/Thatcher bull market of the 1980s, great changes came about, both on Wall Street and in the City of London. A new breed of trader came to the fore and was lionised, especially by those made rich by their trading. A new language grew up with the traders; new definitions of well-known words and phrases entered the language.

Asset stripper   Nothing to do with night clubs, but financial operators who bought companies and sold off their assets, often making thousands redundant.

Blow his tits off   Not sure quite what this meant before, but in Thatcher's world it meant 'sell it to him'. Its converse was 'ship it in shag'.

Butterfly   Pretty only in the sense that it's a no-lose situation in a traded option play.

Chartists   Not forerunners of the unions, but those who predicted future share movements by performance.

Chinese walls   Nothing to do with China, but supposed barriers within the new giant investment banks to prevent the stockbroking side buying shares just before the corporate side announced a takeover they were working on.

Churning   Not your stomach after all the champagne, but the buying and selling of your client's shares for no better reason than it earned you commission.

Concert party Correct – nothing to do with music, but the ganging up of predators before buying shares in a company.

Dog Obvious what a dog is, but in this case it's a share that has performed badly for years. Best example – government War Loan.

Head and shoulders No, not a dandruff treatment but a share shout giving the signal, sell.

Stag By the end of the Thatcher era, at least 9 million new shareholders knew what a stag was – a punter who applied for new issues with the sole intention of selling them instantly.

Being able to understand that made them worth their £250,000 a year, didn't it?

—— Why we should love America ——

In 1945, Europe was shattered and Stalin's Russia was moving west. It had already taken Berlin and, with fascism defeated, communists everywhere were ready to welcome the Red Army. General George Marshall, US Army Chief of Staff during the war, convinced President Truman that American security would be endangered if the European economy collapsed and the communists took over.

The European Recovery Program was put in place, and between April 1948 and June 1952, $13,150,000,000 ($400 billion in today's money) was allocated to what became known as the Marshall Plan, described by Winston Churchill as 'the most unsordid act in history'. Most people have assumed that Germany received the highest allocation, and I can remember people saying in the 1960s and 70s, as the British economy faltered by comparison with Germany: 'Well, of course, they had their factories rebuilt by the Americans.'

The true figures were:

Great Britain	$3,176,000,000
France	$2,706,000,000
Germany	$1,389,000,000

It is one of the great post-war myths that Germany received the most.

———— Are they charitable? ————

Over Christmas 2004 a tsunami struck in Asia, causing widespread damage and loss of life. The British gave no less than £340 million to tsunami appeals in the first two months of 2005.

And many of the wealthy are great givers as well. The good example set by the Carnegie, Rockefeller and Ford foundations is being followed by some of the new wave of fabulously wealthy – notably Bill Gates of Microsoft, whose Gates Foundation, set up with his wife Melinda, is spending and achieving more than many governments.

Another wealthy billionaire is Pierre Omidyar, founder of eBay. He announced in the summer of 2005 a $110 million fund, which will offer start-up finance to companies in the developing world.

Indeed, the Americans, vilified though they may be by many others in the world, are the greatest philanthropists, not only in absolute terms but in relation to their Gross

Domestic Product (GDP). Ms Lagomasino of J.P. Morgan private bank, which runs a global philanthropy forum in which its wealthy clients can exchange ideas, told *The Economist*: 'Americans have a much greater tendency to think about serious philanthropy at much lower levels of wealth. They give away chunks of their money once they are worth around $20 million. Elsewhere it's more like $100 million.'

—— A hundred million, sir? Not —— quite enough, I'm afraid

On 5 May 2004, at the auction house of Sotheby's in New York, a buyer paid a record $104 million for Pablo Picasso's 'Garçon à la Pipe', painted in 1905. It was the first work of art to break the $100 million mark at auction.

The buyer wasn't revealed, but it could have been Andrew 'Jack' Whittaker Jr, who won $314.9 million in the Powerball Lottery on 24 December 2002.

—— £1,200,000,000 – that's just my —— pay-cheque for the year

In October 2005, Philip Green paid himself the largest-ever personal dividend in British corporate history. He took a cool £1.2 billion from his company, Arcadia, the Top Shop to Dorothy Perkins retailing chain he had bought for £850 million in 2002. When he bought it, he put up only £9.2 million in cash (the other £800,000,000 was put up by the bank HBOS).

Peter McKay of the *Daily Mail* seemed to sum it all up rather well:

'HOW GREEN IS OUR ENVY? Rag trade billionaire Philip Green runs the retail group Arcadia, but it is his wife, Tina, who owns 92 per cent of the shares – and to whom he has paid a £1.2 billion bonus. They were introduced twenty years ago. She was married, had two children and found Mr Green "awful". Five years later they were married. "Philip does nothing without consulting me," claims Mrs Green, who says many business decisions are made at the kitchen table of their tax-free home in Monaco. "I can't afford to divorce her," says Mr Green.'

Economy: cutting down other people's wages.

J.B. Morton

McKay went on to speculate on the state of the Green marriage, and whether there might be a pre-nuptial agreement limiting Mrs Green's take in the event of a divorce. He also speculated on whether Philip Green was greedy and concluded that he was, though he conceded that he was also generous, donating heavily to his favourite charities.

Put all your eggs in one basket – WATCH THAT BASKET!

Mark Twain

Anthony Hilton in the *Evening Standard* wasn't so sanguine. In an article entitled 'How Green and Co Reap

Dividends from the Taxpayer', he wrote: 'An important point seems to have been overlooked in the commentary about the £1-billion-plus dividend paid last year by Arcadia to its main shareholder, the wife of Philip Green. It is that roughly two-fifths of the cost of this will fall on the British taxpayer.'

'Arcadia can pay this kind of money because it has taken on debt – essentially mortgaged itself to the banks – using the cashflow coming in every day through the tills as security for the loan. There is nothing new in this. Private-equity houses do it all the time and Mohamed Fayed did it twenty years ago at Harrods/House of Fraser to raise the funds to repay the Sultan of Brunei who had advanced him the original purchase price of the stores group.'

> **Business? It's quite simple. It's other people's money.**
>
> **Alexandre Dumas**

Hilton condemned this deal as non-wealth-creating, financial engineering designed to save the Greens the best part of £400 million in tax. He concluded: 'So when you look at that £1 billion or so taken out by Mrs Green, just remember that you and all the other taxpayers are footing the bill for at least £400 million of it.'

—— It's the Roman Empire again, —— or Here comes Bramo

My middle son supports Chelsea. How pathetic! Anyone can support a team that never loses. Ah, but my son supported them when Roman Abramovich, known — carefully – to his friends as Bramo (or is it Brammo?), was earning £2,000 a year in a remote province of Russia.

Unlike Malcolm Forbes, who puts his talents as a great businessman down to industry and ability (both spelt I-n-h-e-r-i-t-a-n-c-e), Bramo had a rough upbringing. His mother died of blood poisoning when he was eighteen months old, and his father was killed in a building site accident when he was four. He then lived with relatives in Ukhta, a remote oil town almost inside the Arctic Circle. He went to the local industrial institute and then Moscow's Gubkin Institute of Oil and Gas. Already starting to show an entrepreneurial spirit, he sold retread car tyres as a sideline. When perestroika arrived, he set up a company trading in oil products and was noticed by Boris Berezousky, Russia's foremost oil tycoon. Together they bought the oil business Sibneft for £120 million in 1995.

Berezousky was forced into exile and left Bramo in charge of Sibneft. In 2005, Gazprom, the state-controlled Russian natural gas monopoly, bought Sibneft, and Bramo's stake was estimated at £5.1 billion. Sibneft had already paid huge dividends, and Bramo bought Chelsea for £260 million.

He also bought three yachts, including *Pelorus* for which he paid £72 million. For speedier travel he uses his own Boeing 737.

In the year to June 2004, the aggregate pay costs of 124 employees at Chelsea Football Club was no less than £102.5 million, meaning an average of £826,000 per employee.

> *What kind of society isn't structured on greed? The problem of social organisation is how to set up an arrangement under which greed will do the least harm. Capitalism is that kind of system.*
>
> **Milton Friedman**

—— Coins, notes? Give me work —— or tobacco

The Incas living in the Andes mountains survived without money as we know it, i.e. coins, notes, cheques, credit cards. Money meant work, and taxes were paid by working on roads, in the fields, and so on. The rulers paid their subjects in clothing and food. There was plenty of gold and silver, but they were used only for decoration.

Similarly, the tobacco barons of North America didn't pay in money, but rather in tobacco. Clergymen were paid in tobacco until 1758, and wives were bought by colonists with tobacco.

—— Not voted for by the —— taxpayer

If you thought that salaries at the top of the public sector don't match those at the top of the private sector, think again. Here are the top remunerations in the Civil Service in 2004–05.

Organisation	Position	Held by	2003–04 £ total	2004–05 £ total	% increase
Royal Mail	Chief executive of Royal Mail Group	Adam Crozier	814,244	2,726,000	235
Royal Mail	Group finance director	Marisa Cassoni	395,541	1,561,000	295
Royal Mail	Group director, people and organisational development	Tony McCarthy	384,258	1,394,000	263
Royal Mail	Chief executive of Post Office Limited	David Mills	342,889	1,391,000	306
Royal Mail	Group chief, information office	David Burden	N/A	1,054,000	N/A
Network Rail	Chief executive	John Armitt	729,00	919,000	26
British Nuclear Fuels	Chief executive	Michael Parker	595,723	635,711	7
Channel 4	Director of television	Kevin Lygo	473,000	589,000	25
Channel 4	Managing director	David Scott	502,000	588,000	17
Financial Services Authority	Chief executive	John Tiner	471,000	540,252	15
Channel 4	Chief executive	Andrew Duncan	N/A	477,000	N/A
Channel 4	Sales director	Andy Barnes	296,000	464,000	57
BBC	Director-general	Mark Thompson	N/A	459,000	N/A
BBC	Deputy director-general	Mark Byford	384,000	457,000	19
BBC	Chief operations officer	John Smith	327,000	387,000	18
Financial Services Authority	Chairman	Callum McCarthy	382,900	382,448	0
Ofcom	Chief policy officer	Stephen Carter	308,000	347,588	13

Organisation	Position	Held by	2003–04 £ total	2004–05 £ total	% increase
BBC	Director of television	Jana Bennett	305,000	334,000	10
BBC	Director of new media	Ashley Highfield	308,000	320,000	4
Ofcom	Chief policy officer	Kip Meek	258,185	280,178	9
Ofcom	Chief operating officer	Ed Richards	227,891	268,142	18
Bank of England	Governor	Mervyn King	248,301	268,137	8
Cabinet Office	Cabinet Secretary	Sir Andrew Turnbull	215,000	230,000	7
Bank of England	Deputy governor	Sir Andrew Large	217,924	225,584	4
Bank of England	Deputy governor	Rachel Lomax	217,924	225,584	4
Judiciary	Lord Chief Justice	Lord Woolf	205,242	211,399	3
Department of Health	Permanent Secretary	Sir Nigel Crisp	195,000	210,000	8
Cabinet Office	First Parliamentary Counsel	Sir Geoffrey Bowman	200,000	205,000	3
HM Revenue and Customs	Chief information officer	Steve Lamey	N/A	200,000	N/A
Scottish Enterprise	Chief executive	Jack Perry	195,875	197,789	1

Average (excluding Royal Mail)	13.0 per cent
Average (including Royal Mail)	53.2 per cent

This was what Dan Lewis, research director at the Economic Research Council, said: 'We strongly support the idea that the public sector should attract private sector talent, but this government has a track record of always hiring the most expensive management consultants and private sector individuals. The huge salaries were neither voted for by taxpayers nor approved by elected politicians and, worst of all, almost certainly not based on any productivity gains.'

The Office for National Statistics noted that spending on public services increased 65 per cent between 1997 and 2005, while public sector productivity fell by 10 per cent.

—————— Insider dealing ——————

There was a time when insider dealing was legal. You received information from someone in a company, from a stockbroker, a banker or a lawyer, that would affect the share price, and you bought or sold accordingly and *kept quiet about it*. However, the excesses and boastful behaviour of the Thatcher years led to changes in the law, and acting on 'insider' information is now illegal.

> *Rembrandt painted 700 pictures. Of these 3,000 are still in existence.*
>
> **Wilhelm Bode**

Two Daily Mirror journalists who had worked on the paper's City column were convicted of insider dealing and spent their 2005 Christmas holiday contemplating a prison sentence. Their editor, Piers Morgan (sacked for publishing false photographs about torture by British troops in Iraq), was also facing calls for further investigation into his buying and selling of shares in a company called Viglen, which had been tipped in the journalists' column.

The Liberal Democrats' trade spokesman asked Labour's trade minister to look again at Morgan's involvement in the light of what was said at the trial of the two *Mirror* journalists. Morgan referred to one of them, James Hipwell (eventually sentenced to six months in jail), as a 'lying little toe-rag'. And he said on Radio 4's *Today* programme: 'A load of rubbish was said about me on the stand by various people.'

Morgan may well be right that the two journalists lied, but the story that he benefited from their tips refuses to die down.

Civil partnerships

Those specialising in family law will tell you that the marriage and divorce rules apply in a civil partnership. The *Sunday Times* was quick to point out, just before Sir Elton John entered into such a partnership with David Furnish, that any break-up could give Furnish half of John's estimated £185 million fortune, including his magnificent Queen Anne mansion, Woodside, valued at £8 million, his house near Nice in the south of France, worth £3.5 million, a flat on the island of Giudecca near Venice, bought for £1.25 million, and finally John's converted factory in Holland Park, London.

Not that Elton John would probably mind giving plenty away. As the *Sunday Times* also pointed out in its Rich List of 2005, he is the most prolific giver to charitable causes, mainly to his own Aids Foundation. The List calculated that he had given no less than 12 per cent of his wealth, some £22.6 million, in the previous twelve months.

China is coming

At the end of 2005, China announced that its first national economic census had revealed that it was even bigger that it had thought. In fact it was much bigger, to the tune of £170 billion. If this is true, then China has leapfrogged both France and the UK to become the world's fourth-largest economy.

Does it matter? This was the view of the *Financial Times* in mid-December 2005: 'China is more than a fast-growing market. It is a force that, coupled with and magnified by the ongoing revolution in technology, is already changing the world. It has altered the global terms of trade, shifting income from rival producers of light manufactured goods to producers of commodities – including oil – and services.'

'China has put pressure on the wages of low-skilled workers in rich countries, driving up unemployment in countries with inflexible labour markets and increasing differentials … The consumer who enjoys greater spending power, the student who decides it makes sense to get a degree, the investor who ponders whether companies can continue to deliver high returns may not realise that their lives are being shaped in part by China. But they are. That is what the rise of a nation of this size, at this speed, means.'

Staggering pay

The *Guardian* periodically criticises the pay levels and rises of leaders of industry (and trades union leaders do it constantly), but the newspaper kept its sharpest criticism for payment to bankers. On 17 December 2005, in an article with the title 'Staggering Pay on Another Planet', it wrote: 'Hank Paulson, chief executive of Goldman Sachs, will collect $37m (£21m) in pay and share options. He is one of five people at the bank whose remuneration jointly reached $80m (£45m) … On this side of the Atlantic, we wait to see how Bob Diamond fared, but less than £15m for the ambitious head of Barclays Capital would be a surprise … The rewards on offer at investment banks are so much more over-the-top than anything seen these days at large companies, even multinationals. Moreover, the individuals leading the companies – think Lord Browne at BP or J.P. Garnier for British examples – are infinitely more impressive than any banker you'll find.'

> *America's best buy for a nickel is a telephone call to the right man.*
>
> **Ilka Chase**

—— Compound interest ——

After gearing, compound interest is one of the most important expressions in the English language. Suppose you invested £10,000 and were lucky enough to get an interest rate of 5 per cent. Take the interest of £500 each year and it will buy you a nice weekend in Paris for two. Leave it where it is, and this is what happens:

Year	1	the £10,000 becomes	£10,500
	2		£11,020
	3		£11,580
	4		£12,150
	5		£12,760
	6		£13,400
	7		£14,070
	8		£14,770
	9		£15,510
	10		£16,290
	11		£17,100
	12		£17,960
	13		£18,860
	14		£19,800
	15		£20,790
	16		£21,820
	17		£22,920
	18		£24,070
	19		£25,270
	20		£26,530

So, find 5 per cent, leave the money and the interest alone, and in twenty years the £10,000 has become £26,530.

> *I don't know of anything so remorseless on the face of the earth than seven per cent interest.*
>
> **Josh Billings**

In the 1980s, you could get 15 per cent interest with some building societies. Just look at what that does to the same £10,000:

Year 1	the £10,000 becomes	£11,500
2		£13,225
3		£15,209
4		£17,490
5		£20,114
6		£23,131
7		£26,600
8		£30,590
9		£35,179
10		£40,455
11		£46,524
12		£53,502
13		£61,528
14		£70,757
15		£81,371
16		£93,576
17		£107,613

At 15 per cent compound interest, £10,000 becomes £100,000 in less than seventeen years.

What about the kids?

Do the wealthy worry about the effect that their wealth might have on their children? They do. According to a US Trust *Survey of Affluent Americans* published in December 2000, 60 per cent thought it would make their children concentrate too much on material things, 58 per cent thought it would make them naive about money, 55 per cent that they would spend beyond their means, 50 per cent that the affluence would ruin their initiative, and 40 per cent that they would have a hard time taking financial responsibility.

———— Cheque book journalism ————

Big cheques are paid out by newspapers today, usually for some juicy inside story on the sexual and financial shenanigans of a celeb.

It's not new. Before the First World War, Lord North-cliffe, owner of the *Daily Mail*, offered £10,000 (over £1 million) for the first non-stop trans-Atlantic flight. No one achieved it before 1914, but in 1919 Alcock and Brown scooped it in a Rolls-Royce-powered Vimy manu-factured by Vickers.

As long ago as 1895, the *Daily Telegraph* gave the great cricketer W.G. Grace £5,000 (£550,000) for a story.

More serious are the sums paid by newspapers either to convicted criminals or to potential witnesses in court cases. In the Rosemary and Fred West multiple murder cases, Rosemary's lawyers complained that offers of £100,000 had been made to West's family and the relatives of victims. In 1999, Gary Glitter was acquitted after his judge discovered a 'reprehensible' payment by the *News of the World* of £10,000 to a witness, with the promise of £25,000 more on conviction.

Perhaps most notorious of all, in 1979 when the Liberal Party leader, Jeremy Thorpe, was on trial for conspiracy to murder, a key witness, Peter Bessell, was offered £25,000 (about £150,000 today) for his story, and a further £25,000 if Thorpe was convicted.

In finance, when does a human have to take over from a computer? When a large cheque is written.

On 30 March 1995, Glaxo plc wanted to pay Wellcome Trust Nominees Ltd £2,474,655,000 for the Trust's shares in Wellcome plc. The Lloyds Bank computer couldn't produce a cheque for this amount, so a Lloyds employee had to write it by hand. She was so nervous that she had to do it three times before she got it right.

How to earn air miles: in 1995, Eli Broad of Los Angeles bought Roy Lichtenstein's painting 'I ... I'm Sorry' for $2.5 million, paying with his American Express card. It earned him 2.5 million air miles, enough for him to take himself and eight friends to the Moon and back.

While in California, Walter Cavanagh of Santa Clara has 1,397 different credit cards, giving him $1.65 million of credit. He keeps his collection in a wallet 250 feet long.

> *When a man says money can do anything, that settles it: he hasn't any.*
>
> **Edgar Watson Howe**

Sex and the City

In spite of all the legislation, moral pressure and even some highly publicised sexual discrimination cases – a group of female employees at Dresdner, Kleinwort Wasserstein launched a $1.4 billion suit against the bank in late 2005 – women still lag behind men in rewards and positions in business and in the City of London.

The Equal Opportunities Commission reckon it will take Britain 40 years for women to reach parity with men in the boardroom. Currently, in Britain's top 100 companies, 89.5 per cent of the directors are men. Of the 10.5 per cent who are women, just two – Dame Marjorie Scardino, Chief Executive of Pearson, and Baroness Hogg, Chairman of 3i – have truly powerful roles.

Relief in alcohol

Whether related to discrimination or not, the young women of Britain have taken to alcohol in an alarming way. The average amount of alcoholic drink consumed by 18–25-year-old British women – 220 litres per year or four to five bottles of wine a week – is four times more than their Italian counterparts and three times more than their contemporaries in France.

Money and disease

The Max Planck Institute in Germany carried out research into how diseases spread, and to find out how people travelled, they looked at a US website called wheresgeorge.com. Initially set up as a game, the site enables people to register dollar bills after marking them with the website's name. Other users round the world report when they receive a marked bill. The site tracks more than 50 million dollar bills round the world.

For the study, the Planck Institute just tracked 500,000 bills that stayed within the USA. They made some interesting and useful discoveries. After a period of two weeks, 52.7 per cent of bills marked in Seattle were still there, but 7.8 per cent had travelled more than 500 miles. The same percentage applied to those marked in New York.

If we're not careful, we'll all soon be looking at £5 notes and wondering who's transmitting what.

It's only money!

In 1994 the KLF, the Kopyright Liberation Front, burned ONE MILLION POUNDS STERLING on the Isle of Jura in Scotland. The KLF had been one of the seminal bands of the British Acid House movement in the late 1980s and early 90s, and had made a lot of money (nobody seems to be quite sure how much).

When asked why they did it, the two founders of KLF – Jimmy Cauty, otherwise known as Rockman Rock or Lord Rock, and Bill Drummond, alias King Boyd or Time Boy – couldn't give a coherent answer. However, that was in keeping with their approach to life. In 1992, they had left the music industry and deleted their back catalogue. Their exit was spectacular. At the Brit Awards ceremony where they won the award for best group, they killed a sheep and left it at the entrance of the post-awards party. When questioned about this, Drummond said that his original plan was to cut off his hand and throw it into the audience: 'In my head, I was chopping off my own hand and throwing it into the crowds of spectators, claiming the music business for myself.'

Needless to say, a number of people were outraged by this burning of £1 million; some said the money could have been given to the poor. Had the world been made poorer by the burning of a million bits of paper?

—— You wanna pay cost price, —— fine with me

The successful industrialist David Brown decided to buy the luxury car-maker Aston Martin in the 1960s. Like everyone else before and since, he struggled to make it profitable. One of his rich friends decided he would like an Aston Martin, and asked David Brown the price.

'£3,000', he said. (This was in the 1960s. That's £75,000 today.)

'As we're mates, David, couldn't I have one at cost price?' asked his friend.

'Sure', said David Brown, 'that will be £4,000.'

—— Not all French aristocrats —— are poor

Just after the Second World War, Baron Marcel Bich invented the ball-point pen and called it *biro* (correctly pronounced 'birro'). He launched it on $1,000, but within 30 years he was worth $50 million because by then 1,500 million Bic pens a year were being sold, and he received a minute amount on each. However, 1,500 million × a minute amount equals a large amount.

Have the guts, take a percentage

When the costs for the film *Titanic*, made in 1996–7, ran wildly over budget and soared to $200 million, director James Cameron agreed to waive everything except his writer's fee of $1.5 million. The film was a huge success, and by the end of March 1998 had earned more than $1.2 billion at the box office and had won eleven Academy Awards at the Oscars ceremony, including Best Picture and Best Director. Cameron stood to be rewarded with a pay-off of no less than $75–110 million.

A hundred years ago

Life expectancy in the USA was 46 years. Today it's 78 years. Fourteen per cent of American homes had a bath. Marijuana, heroin and morphine were all legal and available at any drugstore. The average worker made between $200 and $400 a year (he makes over $30,000 today).

The population of Las Vegas was 30, and 90 per cent of doctors hadn't been to college.

Finally

Does the present cost of newspapers irritate you? Last Sunday I bought the *Sunday Times*, *Sunday Telegraph*,

Observer and *Mail on Sunday*. The cost was £6.10. When I was at Cambridge in the 1960s, *The Times* cost 6d (2.5p or 50p today), the *Mail* was 2.5d (1.04p or 21p today), and the *Financial Times* 3d (1.25p or 25p today). Newspapers are bigger and, arguably, better – but that much bigger and better?

The Rich:
A New Study
of the Species

William Davis

A light-hearted guide
to the species, *The
Rich* surveys the lives,
loves, foibles, habits,
preferences, hatreds
and much more of the
world's richest people.

William Davis draws
on half a century's
experience in financial
journalism to present a
detailed portrait of the
figures and lives behind

the fortunes – from entrepreneurs like Richard Branson to
sports stars like Tiger Woods, and showbiz legends like Elton
John. He asks:

- What makes them different – are they really a breed
  apart?
- What does it take to amass great wealth, where does it
  come from, and what does it mean to those who have it?
- How do they use their money – and how do they feel
  about the rest of us?
- What is their power – and what are their fears?

The Rich is strongly international, lively and iconoclastic, and
laced with quotes and anecdotes. Thought-provoking and
superbly well-informed, it provides insight into a fascinating
world.

Hardback £16.99

ISBN 10: 1 84046 766 5   ISBN 13: 978 1840467 66 6

What Every Man Wants:
The Ultimate Trophy Book

Andrew Mann

Introduced by
Frankie Dettori

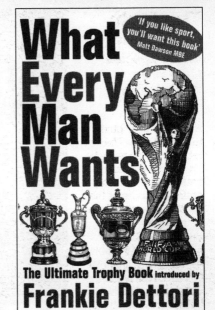

'If you like sport, you'll want this book'
Matt Dawson MBE

The Ryder Cup, the
Ashes, the FA Cup,
the Claret Jug, the
Webb Ellis, the Green
Jacket, the Stanley,
the Americas: men
have always loved
their trophies.

Whatever their game of
choice, winning its ultimate prize is something nearly every
man has dreamed about. Thanks to this brilliant guide to the
most celebrated trophies in the world, he can now get close
enough to almost taste the glory.

What Every Man Wants unearths the essentials on every
revered tournament prize that has ever been fought over in
modern times, including:

- the reasons behind the bizarre codes of sporting conduct
  linked to each trophy
- who you're up against if you want to get involved
- tips on how to collect the silverware
- what can't be found in any rulebook and why it's not just
  the 'taking part' that counts.

Hardback £9.99

ISBN 10: 1 84046 775 4   ISBN 13: 978 1840467 75 8

Places to Hide

Dixe Wills

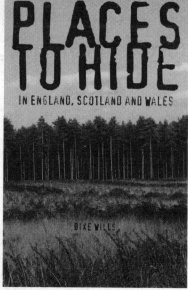

There comes a time in everyone's life when facing up to one's own problems is simply not an option. *Places to Hide* tells you where, precisely, you can escape from the chaos of modern life.

Offering a wide range of hiding places in urban, rural, coastal and mountainous settings throughout Britain, *Places to Hide* is the essential guide to anyone who needs to disappear for a bit.

Those who repeat the mistakes of the past are doomed to forget them, so the experiences of famous hiders such as King Charles II and Lawrence of Arabia are provided in helpful glance-sized chunks to jog the memory of even the most distracted of minds.

With tips on concealment technique, total identity change and crouching, along with up-to-date information on local sources of food, water and camouflage netting, *Places to Hide* is ideal for the professional hider as well as for those who merely wish to hide for pleasure.

Hardback £9.99

ISBN 10: 1 84046 768 1   ISBN 13: 978 1840467 68 0